FOUR
VICTORIAN LADIES
OF
WILTSHIRE

by the same author

★

WITHOUT KNOWING MR. WALKLEY

EDITH OLIVIER

FOUR VICTORIAN LADIES OF WILTSHIRE

with
an essay on
THOSE LEISURED LADIES

FABER & FABER

FOR
ANOTHER VICTORIAN LADY
OF WILTSHIRE
MY SISTER
MARY CARTER

First published in Mcmxlv
by Faber and Faber Limited
24 Russell Square London W.C.1
Second impression June Mcmxlv
Third impression August Mcmxlv
Fourth impression April Mcmxlvi
Printed in Great Britain by
Western Printing Services Limited Bristol
All rights reserved

CONTENTS

ILLUSTRATIONS

ACKNOWLEDGEMENTS

Many people have helped me in writing this book and I would particularly like to mention with gratitude Mrs. G. H. Bell and Messrs. Macmillan for extracts from The Hamwood Papers of The Ladies of Llangollen and Caroline Hamilton, Mr. Reresby Sitwell for a description of the needlework done by Mrs. Jennens; Mrs. Goodman for permission to quote from Mrs. Morrell's *List and Descriptions of Pieces of Work*; Miss Marcia Rice, Lady Grigg, Mrs. Archie Bell, and Miss Dora Martin for some personal memories of Miss Moberly. Lady Gatty for permission to use a Character Sketch of Mrs. Alfred Morrison which was privately published a few years ago. Mrs. Charles Longmore for Diaries and Letters of Miss Townsend and her sisters. Mrs. Guy Wyndham for permission to quote from the Letters of George Wyndham edited by her late husband and for much other help; Mrs. Roger Fulford for Letters written to Mrs. Adeane, and Mrs. Keightley.

EDITH OLIVIER

THOSE LEISURED LADIES

Victorian Ladies would have been astonished to learn that the most advanced modern educationalists consider what they look upon as the 'discovery of leisure' as the opening of a new and critical adventure for the human race, and one which demands a lengthy apprenticeship These clever people are obsessed by their consciousness of the difficult and delicate problem which faces them. It is their task to teach the young how safely they had better approach this strange and restive beast called Leisure, with its completely unaccountable habits; for in this generation there are few who know from personal experience what it might do to its victims. Yet, if the moderns were only aware of it, the most fearless teachers of the dreaded sport would be their own grandmothers and great-aunts, though those ladies might wonder why so much fuss should be made over anything so everyday. They always had leisure enough and to spare, and no-one ever taught them how to use it. That idea would have seemed to them as ridiculous as 'taking lessons' in the art of holding a tiny hinged and fringed parasol at the best angle for keeping the sun off the face; or of laboriously learning rhythmically to sway an enormous feather fan in order to cool the air. For Victorian ladies such things were instinctive. Leisure was the substance of their lives, and upon this firm and unchanging foundation they embroidered their own peculiar pattern.

What then is Leisure?

Those Leisured Ladies

The *Oxford Dictionary* of course supplies us with the complete definition. Leisure is 'Freedom or opportunity to do something. An opportunity. Opportunity offered by unoccupied time.' We have then here something which is far from suggesting unemployment. Leisure is a living thing—a starting-point. The Dictionary continues by quoting some words written by Sir William Temple, the seventeenth-century diplomatist: 'the Desire of Leisure is much more Natural than that of Busyness and Care'. Our Victorian ladies were both leisurely and natural, but this does not mean that they were idle. They possessed the 'opportunity to do something', and they chose their own employment. Here is the true distinction between Labour and Leisure. The one is imposed from without: it bears with it Busyness and Care. The other is self-selected occupation: it is therefore natural.

Victorian ladies were indeed busy, but they chose upon what they would be busy. They sometimes seem to us to have been absurdly sentimental, dreaming their dreams, and overflowing with their ideals; but those dreams of theirs were not idle dreams. They came 'through the multitude of business', and their business, in turn, was inspired by their dreams. Florence Nightingale and Octavia Hill are the ideal Victorian Ladies, and in each of them, the Dream and the Business became one. Those two women are the summit of Victorianism, for neither could have been produced by any other Age. Leisure was, first of all, essential to create those personalities—thoughtful, idealistic, and surprisingly practical when their training had been so eminently unpractical. They simply were not aware of the difficulties lying between them and what they set out to do. They had no experience of details. Each of them merely saw that certain work must be done, and each flung herself into it. Leisure had given them the opportunity to choose their own occupations, and the ones they chose were so overwhelming that henceforth they had no further leisure, and no further choice.

Our four Victorian Ladies did not reach such heights as these, but they were none the less true to their time. More so, in one way, for ladies like themselves might have been found in many other neighbourhoods during those years. I have chosen these four, because they all happened to live at the same time and in the same bit of country—the twenty miles which lie between Salisbury and

East Knoyle. Their characters were typical of the days when Leisure bordered Life like the margin of a well-printed page. And as on that page, the effect produced was one of space, dignity, and beauty, in the midst of which was set the main purpose of the book. The story told is not one of sudden sharp changes, or of surprising events. As a rule, the leisured life moved easily, one day flowing out of the day before; and if anything unexpected did occur, it was absorbed into the calm rhythm of a life for ever impelled by an impetus from the past.

During the nineteenth century the feminine population of Wiltshire was neither more nor less Victorian than was the case in other counties. Only one generalization can fearlessly be made about the ladies in every county in England. They were not mass-produced. If we look back at them, from a distance of half a century or more, they may appear to have been so, but that is simply a question of dress. When I speak of dress, I am not only thinking about clothes. I include all the paraphernalia which combine to make up outward appearance—the rooms in which the Victorians lived, with their furniture, antimacassars, tea cosies, and knick-knacks; the clothes they wore; the games they played; and their social habits in general.

We know what those were from the pictures in *Punch*. Here we see the people of the day driving, sitting, and walking in Hyde Park; we see them at Races and archery meetings, at croquet and lawn-tennis parties, and dinners, and what-not. The *Punch* drawings are perfectly true representations of one side of the life they depict, but, far less than would be the case to-day, do they cover that life as a whole. They illustrate the hours which the Victorians spent in Society, and that life is obliged to be a standardized one, people following the same fashions and doing the same things, but those things took a very small proportion of the lives of Victorians. The rest was spent in the retirement of family life, when they were free to dress and do as they pleased.

The clothes of the *Punch* ladies were true to Victorian fashions, whether crinoline, bustle, or polonaise; and outwardly their lives followed a more conventional routine than those lived by their present-day successors. Country life was much the same in most country houses. This was part of the good manners of the day. Most ladies played whist, consequences, and the piano. If they were young and active, they also played lawn tennis and rounders. If they were tall and graceful, they shot with bows and arrows. Whatever their figures, they took part in charades and private theatricals. They did not do all this primarily for love of the things themselves, but because to do them was part of the duty of entertaining. Young ladies were put to some trouble to learn the games which their guests might wish to play. The manners of each generation are the language they speak in common with the people they meet in society, and to learn the fashionable games was to learn the A B C of good manners. Such games might be called a sort of 'Basic English', artificial and easy to learn, though not carrying one very far. But the truest pictures of Victorian life were not in *Punch*. Old family photograph books tell us far more, for the long periods which these people spent with their families took much more of their lives than the hours that they spent in society. To-day we cannot realize what it must have meant to spend months on end in the family circle, but it was that which made the Victorians so individual. In those practically uninterrupted months, they had the time and the inclination to follow their private tastes and pursuits. Like *Candide* they found that the last word spoken by philosophy is that *il faut cultiver notre jardin*, and in this absorbing and isolating occupation they spent the greater part of their time.

Victorian Leisure was a by-product of Victorian Riches, and, if only for that reason, we cannot expect to look upon its like again. The richer classes accepted the adjective of 'leisured' as appropriate to themselves. Now it would be considered insulting, for, in the casual vocabulary of to-day, leisure is often used as a polite word for laziness. Really, many people do desire laziness rather than leisure, for in the rush of the modern world we are reaching the last desire of the old woman who asked that her epitaph might be

' *I am going to do nothing for ever and ever*'.

But if we give the word its true meaning and then look back upon the leisurely age of our predecessors, we shall find that leisure encouraged a host of pleasant intimate things, beginning with such childish pleasures as making toast by the schoolroom fire, or roasting chestnuts in the ashes after supper. From these beginnings fol-

lowed many other intimacies, mostly connected with the family,
which then was much more of a close corporation than it is to-day.
People were really intimate with hardly anyone but their parents,
brothers, and sisters. The morning post was family property, and
many letters were read aloud at the breakfast table. The father of
the family took most seriously his office of high priest, reading
daily prayers before breakfast every morning, and in the evening
there was often more reading aloud—a leading article from *The
Times* of the day, or the current number of a Dickens novel. After
luncheon on Sundays, large family parties walked round the stables,
accompanied by a groom carrying bunches of carrots, or a sieve full
of apples for the favourite horses. Sunday was in fact a great day for
group walks, as few other pastimes were tolerated. Week-end
parties did not come into vogue until Queen Victoria had been for
some time on the throne, and in many houses they were at first
limited to relations. This reduced their size and so saved the servants from carrying upstairs too many cans of water in the early
morning, or from emptying too many baths after breakfast.

It is a pity that many people living now, who believe that they
can remember Victorian Sundays, recall them as infinitely boring.
Why was a week-end with the grandparents something to be
dreaded as it approached, and to be rejoiced over in retrospect?
The answer probably is that these memories date back only to the
last decade of the nineteenth century, when the age of leisure, which
had created the Victorian Sunday technique, was already a thing of
the past. The people who assembled for these fleeting week-ends
were already out of touch with the world which had grown up
among these customs. For the *fin de siècle* Victorians (as they liked
to call themselves) it was already a world of the past. Its inhabitants had been accustomed to spend months in each year solely in
each other's company; and their views on everything—religion,
politics, Sunday observance and the rest, were entirely in accord.
After spending leisurely weeks under the same roof, each busy with
his own self-selected occupations, they had found it infinitely pleasant to pass a quiet and sacred day together. Sunday was for them a
Day of Rest.

But the late Victorians rejoiced to know that 'nous avons
changé tout celà'. They arrived for their week-end from a world in

which the pace had already been greatly quickened, and they came from a high sense of duty. They had resolved, from affection for their parents or grandparents, to make the best of what they knew was bound to be a dull Sunday; and, in order to make this best, they often obtained permission to bring with them a few friends. These outside guests made an inappropriate fringe on the outer edge of what would, in any case, have been a loosely compacted fraternity. It had not always been explained to them that they would be dragged out of bed in the small hours of the morning, to meet in the hall at a quarter to eleven on the way to the village church. They resented this. And it did not amuse them, after luncheon, to watch the horses scrunching and slobbering in the loose box over the apples and carrots. They expected, at least, to be allowed to play bridge after dinner, for by then the sacred rites of the holy day were presumably ended, and grandpapa was quite aware of this. His only concession to this unspoken, but not unconcealed, desire was that he sacrificed his favourite practice of reading aloud to the family for an hour after dinner, but he allowed nothing else to take its place. So the evening dragged slowly and wearily by, the silence interrupted only by an occasional snore from grandfather himself.

To appreciate Victorian leisure, we must clear our minds of this mongrel version of it, and forget the period when it had overflowed into the age of speed. The two clashed, and each spoiled the other. No-one can realize what true leisure meant, unless they can reconstruct a picture of it when it was in undisturbed possession.

Fortunately we can do this by studying its most characteristic product—the letters of the time. An age of leisure creates anew the art of letter-writing; and the art of letter-writing in its turn recreates for future generations an age of leisure.

In the eighteenth and nineteenth centuries this art reached its zenith, and it opens for us a doorway into a world in which a kindred art, the art of Intimacy, was also at its height. The letters of many well-known persons have been published and they form a most enjoyable branch of literature; but there are also in most houses (or were until the days of salvage drives) many boxes of old family letters describing in detail the world which existed behind the scenes of the *Punch* drawings. For these writers nothing is insignificant. Every day lives again. On the fine ones, we hear of gardening and country walks: on the wet ones, we are told of books and needlework. There are descriptions of how the great family clans hung together. We read of long visits paid by grandfathers and grandmothers, uncles, aunts, and cousins who arrive complete with nurses, ladies' maids, governesses, footmen, coachmen, horses and carriages. They stayed for weeks or even months; and it is no wonder that the seventeenth century Rectory of Chilmark in Wiltshire was in Queen Victoria's day increased by a wing larger than the original house. Mrs. Lear, the rector's wife, writes of family parties of fifteen, with all their servants as well, descending upon the rectory for the whole of the summer. George Herbert's little parsonage at Bemerton was almost doubled in size during the nineteenth century. This was to enable the four cultivated daughters of the rector to find space for the practice of their various talents. Their rectory blossomed into studios, music rooms, and parish rooms.

In the diary of the Townsend sisters the cryptic word '*Dis*' often occurs as the occupation of the afternoon. This syllable stood for *district visiting*, for Victorian ladies who lived in the country (and most of them did) made friends, as a matter of course, with their cottage neighbours. They combined this with the prevalent fashion for walking. In their long skirts, their pork-pie hats, and their buttoned kid walking boots, they tramped many a long mile during their afternoons; and readers of *The Daisy Chain* will remember that they always wanted an "*object*" for their walks. In that book there were expeditions nearly every day to Cocksmoor; and on one great day, not only did Mr. Wilmot, Richard, Ethel, and Margaret, set out on foot 'directly after dinner' but Flora drove Blanche and Audrey to meet them in the gig, carrying cakes, tea kettles, and prizes. The May family preferred to move in swarms, for before another expedition to Cocksmoor, when Mr. Earnescliffe discovered that only six persons had 'gathered in the hall', he exclaimed in horror, 'Is this all the walking party?' Apologies were made for the non-appearance of another four, and so the diminished party set out.

Few Victorians started on these regular walks of theirs unprovided with a basin of soup to be carried to some bed-ridden person living within any distance up to two or three miles away. There were in those days a surprising number of bed-ridden people in all spheres of life, and they were ever ready 'objects' for walks. Another was some little child who was not able to get to the nearest school, and Victorian ladies walked long distances to teach these isolated pupils how to read and write and to say the catechism.

Sketching was another accepted 'object' for a country walk, for these leisured ladies did not satisfy their artistic tastes only by visiting the Royal Academy. They practised the arts themselves, being entirely free from the modern horror of the word 'amateur'. In fact it was one of their favourite words. They used it in its original or root meaning: 'one who loves, or has a taste for anything, or cultivates it as a pastime'.

It must be confessed that leisure combined with a taste for amateurishness has been responsible for a good many parodies of the arts. The fact that a lady has leisure enabling her to choose her own occupations, need not mean that everything that she does will be worth doing from the aesthetic point of view. Leisure cannot take the place of talent: it can only give opportunity for its use. During the twenty years or so before Barbara Townsend was born, there lived in a house nearly adjoining Mompesson, a lady named Miss Child. She might be described as an 'amateur of Salisbury Close' for she 'loved it, had a taste for it, and cultivated it as a pastime'. Since her day, there have been many residents in the Close who shared this taste of hers, for to be an amateur of a place is as active an impulse as to be an amateur of any of the arts.

Miss Child was neither poet nor historian, but she was an ardent humble amateur in both directions. She collected the legends and traditions of Salisbury and its Cathedral, in the spirit of an uncritical and simple-minded old gossip, and this is indeed what she was. Some time in the 'forties she made a number of these stories into a lengthy local epic, written in the rhymed couplets which (in common with other people at the time) she believed could of themselves make any writing into poetry. Her book was called:

THE SPINSTER AT HOME IN THE CLOSE OF SALISBURY

NO FABLE

She opened by bidding her verses to

> *Crave lenient forbearance to errors of style,*
> *Suggest that 'tis gracious at follies to smile*

Those Leisured Ladies

After this, who could smile otherwise than graciously? And when Miss Child modestly hopes

> *That historical facts may be useful to youth,*
> *And the faults of poor rhymes be excused for their truth,*

one is given an improving motive for leniency.

What Miss Child did was to preserve some old Salisbury stories which without her might have been forgotten; but unfortunately she was a bad versifier, and the legends lose a good deal by their translation into her jog-trot medium. The real value of her book is in its unconsciously drawn picture of the writer's world. She set out to tell of the gallant days of chivalry, and of the pomp and splendour of the medieval church, but these high themes are shown as they were imagined in the mind of a 'Spinster at home in the Close' of the eighteen-forties. A third edition of the poem (for it went through several), was dedicated to those 'very numerous patrons whose merry meetings have so often enlightened her boudoir'. She says that these meetings took place in her

> *tiny abode, well befitting a Spinster*
> *In a nook of the Close, which belongs to its Minster.*
> *I can look from my window and see the west end*
> *Of that glorious pile which we all must commend.*

And here is Miss Child, describing her own life in that nook:

> *I have friends, too, who frequently ask me to dine,*
> *When I taste of choice viands and sip the best wine;*
> *But full oft I decline these kind invitations,*
> *Of my home being fond and my own meditations.*
> *On my sofa I lounge with illustrious dead,*
> *And rejoice there are so many books to be read.*
> *I've sharp-pointed needles, a well-polished thimble*
> *To enweave slender threads with fingers right nimble:*
> *I've long letters to read, and still longer to write,*
> *In my mansion must see all things burnished and bright,*
> *Wherein summers and winters eighteen I have spent,*
> *With spring also and autumn, in peace and content,*
> *Oblivious never to the strict day of rent.*

Those Leisured Ladies

The manner is arid, and it is hard to believe that Miss Child's meetings with her friends were ever particularly merry. She obviously had few gifts, but even so, she enjoyed her leisure, asking for no lessons in the art of using it. It is fair to quote her, because it is sometimes said that the leisured age was all very well for distinguished amateurs or for women of outstanding gifts, as time would never hang heavy on their hands, and they would know how to use it. But the instance of Miss Child proves that even a rather tiresome kind of mind was then free to develop itself as far as it could go. It was not frustrated by the fear of falling below any standard of mass production surrounding it. Again the individual was respected.

Two of the Victorian ladies who will be described in this book lived in Salisbury Close only a few years later than Miss Child. Outwardly their lives must have been much like hers, but they were really gifted amateurs, which is quite another thing, and where such people exist in any number, the soil is prepared for the arts.

It might almost be said that great art requires great amateurs as a background. The singer must have his understanding audience; the writer demands a reader: the painter or sculptor is stimulated by the appreciative eyes which will welcome his masterpiece. How otherwise can one explain the apparently sudden uprushes of genius which occur in certain generations? The Athenians of the fifth century were worthy of their Sophocles and Aeschylus, of their Praxiteles, their Socrates, and their Plato. It is said that the country receives the government it deserves. More so is this the case with art. Think of Europe at the close of the so-called 'dark ages' when the flood of Germanic barbarism had swept over the Roman civilization. It is often assumed that there was no art between this Decline and Fall and the Renaissance; but in reality it never was more universal. Those centuries saw Europe overwhelmed by barbarians; then came the successive Crusades, and then the long series of European wars while the nations of to-day were emerging. One feels that everyone in Europe must have been occupied with this fighting, at least so we think, with our slogan 'Don't you know there is a war on?' Yet during those years the whole of Europe, from the northern borders of Ireland and Scotland to the Golden Horn at its south-eastern limits, blossomed into cathedrals, abbeys, and great religious houses.

Those Leisured Ladies

Within and around these buildings could have been found a host of artists known and unknown. The paintings in the catacombs are said to go back to the days when the gospels were actually being written, and the following centuries saw the creation of the colossal mosaics of Santa Sophia and the great Byzantine and Romanesque churches. Painters covered walls with frescoes, and painted altar pieces and chapel pictures. There were the great glass painters of Chartres, of Fairford, and of York, and the sculptors who filled Amiens with its exquisitely beautiful and touching wood carvings; or clothed the west front of Salisbury Cathedral with an army of saints, destroyed by later iconoclasts. Monks in their cells illuminated missals and gospel books. Nuns and ladies were busy with their tapestry, or embroidered vestments, and hangings for the altar. And in the churches, cathedrals, and abbeys could be heard the austere magnificent music composed for the church services between the days of Pope Gregory and Palestrina. When one realizes how small was then the whole population of Europe, and looks upon this bewildering legacy of the Middle Ages, it seems that Blake's words must then have come true, and that every Christian at the time was a painter, a musician, or an architect.

The background of leisured minds needed by these flourishing arts was fostered by the Benedictine Order; and in this country at least, the Reformation ended its widespread influence. Leisure then became the prerogative of the upper classes and for them the climax of the leisured age came in the eighteenth and nineteenth centuries.

The famous Ladies of Llangollen cannot be called Victorian, for they both died in the decade before the Queen came to the throne, yet the story of their surprising and adventurous experiment is the best of preludes to the study of the ladies of leisure in any generation. In 1788, Lady Eleanor Butler and Miss Sarah Ponsonby fled together from a society which bored them, to a remote cottage in the Denbighshire mountains. From the day they settled there until their deaths about fifty years later, neither of the ladies slept for a single night away from their chosen home. Nevertheless they had no wish to leave the world behind. They looked for, and found, the freedom of choice which is inherent in true leisure. They 'received' a large number of visitors, but they exercised the right of being very fastidious as to whom they did receive. The chief things they asked of their guests were that they should not stay too long, or interrupt too much the even tenor of life at Plas Newydd. They were truly amateurs of leisure, making its practice into a fine art.

Plas Newydd lies beside the road from London to Holyhead, and on their journeys to and from Ireland, most of the well-known people of the day turned off to visit the ladies. Statesmen like Pitt and Burke were their intimates; Arthur Wellesley, 'a charming young man, handsome, fashioned tall and elegant, stayed till two' on his first visit. He remained their friend till many years later when, as the great Duke of Wellington, he helped them with grants from the Civil List, for they had very little money of their own.

Among the charms of a leisured life in a country place is that one is not dependent for society on the occasional visits of famous people who, to tell the truth, are rare birds of passage in any age and any neighbourhood. Leisure in the country means the opportunity of getting to know people of all kinds.

The Ladies of Llangollen made the best use of this opportunity. One morning they 'got two plates of cherries, one white, the other the Orleans cherry, for breakfast. Threw them in a careless manner over the library table, which had a beautiful effect. The Bishop of Saint Asaph, Mrs. Shipley, two Miss Shipleys came. Examined our vines, melons, and mushroom bed, our back-yard, fowl-yard, stable and dairy. Then returned to the Library. Looked over our books and drawings. They staid till one. We felt quite sorry when they took leave. A most charming and wonderfully accomplished family, perfect mistresses of Latin, Italian, French, and painting.'

Another day a note came: 'Mr. and Mrs. de Luc who were just arrived. Sent to invite them up immediately. Very agreeable charming couple. Subjects of conversation: the Emperor, troubles in France, character of the Queen of France, Louis XVI, Monsieur, account of Lavater, of the German language, Noble Institutions in the Protestant Dominions of Germany, like monasteries without their abuses.'

From these supremely cultivated guests the ladies turned to 'a crowd of people, the attendants of a wedding from Wrexham, who entreated permission to see the shrubbery. Could not refuse them permission on this most probably happiest day of their lives.

MRS. PERCY WYNDHAM
from the drawing by G. F. Watts in the possession of Mrs. Guy
Wyndham

A MORNING AT GUNDIMORE: VICTORIAN YOUNG LADIES ENJOY
THEIR LEISURE

from a watercolour by Barbara Townsend in the sixties

Looked at them as they walked. Very well dressed in a plain clean way, befitting their station in life.'

Then again, 'Our landlord Mr. Richard Griffiths and the Clerk ploughing, sowing, harrowing and limeing the field before our cottage. No words can describe the sweetness, the festivity of the scene, the brilliancy of the day, the beauty of the country. The fields so animated. The number of workmen, the various implements of husbandry, as carts, plough, harrow, and sacks of corn together formed a picture of rural content that monarchs might behold with envy.'

Another day, came a 'loud rap at the door. Gentleman from Ireland desired to speak with us. Sent to inquire his name. Frizzle. Desired him to walk in. Never saw him before. Good sort of man. Agent to Mr. Kavanagh. The very essence of vulgarity, a perfect comedy worthy of Foote, affectation of taste and science, but underneath this fantastic husk I believe there lies a good heart.'

They were not uncritical or promiscuous. 'A clergyman came with (as he says) compliments and inquiries from Lord Ormonde. Returned thanks to Lord O., but declined seeing the reverend gentleman.' Again, 'in our absence three nameless ladies came to see the place, two foreign gentlemen and Humphries of Shrewsbury. Forsooth.' And one day 'Met the Vicar. Invited him to coffee. The good man more stupid than ever. Incredible and impossible as that appeared to us last time we saw him.'

One last acquaintance: 'The Thatcher came, a snuffy, sauntering, lazy creature. I am persuaded he is a vile workman . . . sent William Jones, and the sauntering Thatcher to the Mountain for hazel rods to bind the thatch . . . think the Thatcher horrible. Told him so. Fought him . . . The large-faced Carpenter made a frame for the pendant sides of the shed. The little workman bound them with the hazel. The Thatcher who had nothing to recommend him as a workman but simplicity, good humour, and a good complexion, went on clumsily with his job.'

Though the Ladies never slept away from home, they had leisure to travel distances which sound amazing for those days of only horse transport. On a 'delicious morning' in August they rose at four, and 'set out in the Lyon chaise and four', for a day's sightseeing. They travelled for miles through wild rough mountain country and at last came across a harvest festival where 'the reapers were spending the evening, or rather night, in mirth and conviviality'. In spite of their early start, the Ladies stayed to listen while this party 'sang many songs, all applicable to their situation, in praise of a farmer's life, some hunting songs, and one on Lord Hawke. We are quite delighted with the excellence of their voices. Returned home by a delicious moon. Arrived at one.'

But the pleasures of solitude were the sincerest pleasures of all, in this life which was lived in the spirit of the verse decorating the title-page of Lady Eleanor's Journal:

> *Society is all but rude*
> *To this delicious solitude,*
> *Where all the flowers and leaves do close*
> *To weave the garland of repose.*

And in spite of all their visitors, the following extracts describe their happiest hours.

'Spent the evening without candles, by the light of the fire, and faint glimmering of a pale moon, talking over our affairs. My sweet love. A silent pensive day.' And on another day they 'rose at seven. Delicious soft grey morning. If it would but continue fair! Rooks cawing, sheep bleating, rush of waters, weavers' loom, village bell tolling. Such an assembly of rural noises.' And then again: 'From half-past six till nine read Rousseau to my beloved. She working her cross-stitch.'

It might be thought from Lady Eleanor's diaries that the life of the Ladies of Llangollen was little beyond a *dolce far niente*, but this was not the case. They were never idle. Their staff of servants was small, and they did almost as much of the work of their house, farm, and garden as is done in these days of war by the many women who to-day are left to 'carry on' alone. When the Ladies took the Bishop of Saint Asaph to see their dairy, fowl-yard, and melon and mushroom beds, they were showing him really what were the main occupations of their days.

And then there was Sarah's cross-stitch.

Ladies of leisure have always done quantities of fine needlework, and one sometimes wonders how they could have crowded into the hours of daylight the work required by the astonishing number of pieces they have left to us. Perhaps in order to make the best use of artificial light, some of the eighteenth-century embroidresses used the lace-maker's lamp. This was a glass globe filled with water and fixed on to a stand, which was placed between the candle and the piece of work. It strengthened the light, concentrating it on to that part of the work which was actually being carried out, and all this without any glare. In fact there is no strong light so soothing as that from one of these lamps, and though they have been superseded by electric light, they have certainly not been excelled.

In what she called her 'southern parlour' at Weston Hall in Northants during the forty-six years between 1714 and 1760, Mrs. Susanna Jennens must have sat by the window for many more hours than those in which the sun shone. Otherwise she could never have achieved the work she has left behind. In 1713 she was left a widow at the age of twenty-five, and in the following year her father, Sir John Blencowe, gave her as a valentine a beautiful little manor house on his estate, Weston Hall. Mrs. Jennens at this time had three children under five. She loved her children: she loved her valentine: she loved her sewing. Those three things were to fill the rest of her life. Her future was settled. It must have been peaceful, happy, and creative.

I quote from a letter lately written by a son of the present owner of Weston Hall:

'Of her needlework there is much that remains. In the room over the library or "southern parlour" as Mrs. Jennens calls it, there remain fine proofs of her beautiful embroidery. Six of the eight oak chairs she covered with needlework survive, and curtains of the same design are still hanging. The carpet she made has been removed owing to the wear and tear of two centuries. But the best specimens of her art remain, in the beautiful curtains and ceiling of the four-poster. These have, in common with her six chairs and two window curtains, a dark mauve or violet background studded with flowers of all sorts, rather larger than real life. Old-fashioned roses, sunflowers, chrysanthemums, tulips, lilies, etc., either in bunches as on most of the backs of the chairs, or arranged in graceful wreaths and ringlets. The back of the bed has a superb basket of flowers, like that on one of the chairs, surmounted by a flowery wreath. On the back cover above this are two golden pillars entwined with more flowers. Besides these works, Mrs. Jennens made several feather pictures and the fire screen.'

When Harriette Anne Morrell died in 1924, she left behind her an exquisitely written and decorated 'List and Description of pieces of work begun and finished by me' after the year 1870. It is in itself a pretty piece of work, but it commemorates eighty-seven still prettier pieces of painting and needlework. 'There are several large painted screens, babies' sashes, pictures, chairs, cushions, quilts, fans, and jewelled book-covers. The List is charmingly illustrated, and the little accounts of each piece include not only its details, but its destination. They tell whether it was made as a gift or sold for a charity. It contains also some of the mottoes with which she loved to besprinkle her work, like 'Chacun fait à sa manière le rêve de sa vie'; or 'Patience passe science'—surely the prettiest and most playful of puns.

Like many Victorian ladies, Harriette Anne Morrell had in her life only two homes—her father's and her husband's. Both were in Oxford. She was born in Saint John's College, of which her father was President; and the last sixty years of her life were spent in Black Hall, her husband's fine Jacobean house in Saint Giles'. On my first visit to Oxford, I saw outside this house a State Coach, and within it the august figure of a Judge attended by his Marshal, and surrounded by a glittering Cavalry escort. I learnt that every year the Judge on Circuit thus broke in upon the cultured leisure of the occupants of the Saint Giles' houses. Such splendid interruptions were all in the day's work in the spacious days of the past, and Mrs. Morrell's great output of work was in no way affected by the fact that her house was neighboured by the 'Judge's Lodgings'.

In that thought of the sense of continuity lies one secret of the leisured life, giving to it much of its calm security. It also makes it very difficult to recapture in these modern days, in spite of the training for leisure so honestly offered by our educationalists. That old leisure was rooted in the past and was well aware of it. The complete Victorian was proud of his grandparents. He was proud of succeeding to their ideas as well as to their estates. He liked to know that he had inherited their politics and their religion, and that these too were deeply rooted in the countryside. For centuries past, in the convent garden, its cloisters and its cells, in the cathe-

Those Leisured Ladies

dral close and the little country town, in the farming village and in the great house in the park, the individual had grown to maturity as the 'foster-child of silence and slow time'. The memories of all of this were still alive in the nineteenth century. Perhaps the Victorian ladies were the last of a dying race.

MISS
ANNIE MOBERLY

Two patron saints must have presided over Annie Moberly's child-hood and youth—Anthony Trollope and Charlotte Yonge. Trollope was unaware of his influence, although his books were then ardently read by everyone in the clerical world; but Charlotte Yonge was the friend, godmother, teacher, and playmate of the whole Moberly family.

The society described by these two writers was that in which Annie Moberly grew up; and the world they wrote about combines with their manner of writing to make their books the complete expression of all that we imagine life to have been in clerical and county society, during the fifties and sixties of the last century.

More than this. Geographically, Annie Moberly was herself a native of Barsetshire, that imaginary county including those parts of Wiltshire and Hampshire which lie around their respective cathedral cities.

Trollope himself has told us how, when like Tennyson at Coventry, he once 'waited for the train' at Salisbury, he too 'hung upon the bridge' to 'watch the spire'. As he did so he saw the brothers of Saint Nicholas Hospital moving about their garden and round the house of their warden, which looks upon the Avon as it leaves the close. In that half-hour there first stirred in his mind a germ which would later come to life in a series of novels immortalizing Mr. Harding, Mrs. Proudie, Archdeacon Grantley, and the society in which they lived. Later on, memories of Saint Cross at Winchester enriched the picture, but that does not take it out of Miss Moberly's world, for she was born in Winchester College, and lived till middle life in the palace at Salisbury. She was as much a native of Barsetshire as was Mrs. Proudie.

When Annie came upon the scene, Charlotte Yonge was already a personage in the Winchester neighbourhood, and she had been for some years a close friend of the Moberlys. It used to be said that the enormous family of Dr. May in *The Daisy Chain* was drawn from Dr. Moberly's family of fifteen; and my mother, who knew them all very well, always declared that Annie was the original of the Bluestocking Ethel. However, Miss Moberly herself has recorded that 'the family in *The Daisy Chain* was given the name of *May* in honour of our baby (Miss Yonge's godchild) and the large family in the book had been suggested by the party of Miss Yonge's own cousins at Puslinch'. Certainly, there were in those days so many families of fifteen that more than the mention of their number would be needed to identify them.

Charlotte Yonge's careful prose sounds very sedate in the ears of this generation. To write to-day as she did eighty years ago would mean being completely out of touch with contemporary youth, but formality was in the air breathed by everyone about her. They read her rather prim books as naturally as she wrote them. In her day, she was both learned and scholarly, but she also enjoyed the fun and amusements of her generation. The Moberlys liked acting: Miss Yonge liked writing plays. She also liked designing theatrical dresses, making them, and even wearing them. She liked 'stage managing', as they then called what we call 'producing'. When one of the Moberly brothers absolutely refused to be a Roundhead colonel in one of her plays, Miss Yonge dressed up her old mother in the costume and made her play the part.

As children, the Moberlys often stayed with the Kebles at Hursley, and in this house they found a mixture of gaiety and gravity, of 'plain living and high thinking', which is not often seen to-day. Annie Moberly spoke somewhere of 'the self-controlled vivacity of high spiritual existence' which she saw about her in childhood; and she could not imagine why anyone thought that the country life of people like the Kebles 'must have been quiet almost to dullness'. Quiet, possibly, but not dull.

Now we come to the Moberly parents themselves, and they were by no means ordinary. I am coming to think that, in Victorian days, nobody was.

The words 'a Victorian bishop' call up a very definite picture in the mind, statesmanlike, dignified, dogmatic, and mundane. We feel we know what they were all like—consecrated Mr. Gladstones. But throughout those sixty years there·was surely only one occupant of the Bishops' Bench who was also a descendant of Peter the Great. It is another Victorian surprise.

I did not see Miss Moberly's pedigree till after her death, and in her lifetime she never admitted to any Russian connection beyond the fact that her father's grandfather was John Cayley, the British Consul at Petersburg. Her Slavonic appearance suggested something more racial. With her straight black hair, dark eyes, high cheek bones, pale face, and square figure, she had never seemed either episcopal or academic. She was now proved to be dynastic. The Dictionary of National Biography records that when, towards the end of the seventeenth century, the Tsar Peter came to work in the shipyards of Greenwich he there fell in love with a shipmaster's daughter by whom he had three children. They were Alexander Cozens the well-known miniaturist and portrait painter, the Russian General Peter Cozens, and Richard Cozens, a naval constructor at Kronstadt. It was Richard's daughter Sally who married John Cayley.

Mrs. Moberly was painted as a girl by Sir David Wilkie, and as an old woman by George Richmond. Both portraits show her to have been exquisitely beautiful. She too came of no settled Anglo-Saxon stock. Her parents were Scotch, and, like the Moberlys, her family was in the consular service. She was brought up in Leghorn where her various Campbell and Maclean relations used to foregather to sing Gaelic songs and to tell Highland stories. When she grew up, Mary Anne Crokat was known as 'the Beauty of Naples' where she first came out; and she afterwards danced her gay way into the most exclusive Genoese society. She found England rather *triste* when she first returned here after that sunlit and romantic Italian life; but she soon married and was supremely happy, although marriage in her case did indeed mean 'settling down'. So humbly did she settle that, in all her married life, there is only one recorded instance of her daring to call her husband by his Christian name. To the end, she remained the most beautiful woman, and one of the loveliest of my own memories was being taken to see her when I was a child of thirteen. She was lying in bed in her house in Salisbury. Her skin had still the transparency of a girl of eighteen, her hands were very delicate and white, and a lace cap was placed upon her white hair.

Annie Moberly's background, then, was a 'Landscape with Figures'—the landscape Trollopian, and the figures mostly by Miss Yonge. It is, therefore, not to be wondered at that its living inhabitants were a great many bishops and archbishops, a sprinkling of deans and archdeacons, the headmasters of most of the English public schools, Winchester boys past and present, university graduates and undergraduates, and contemporary women writers, including, beside Miss Yonge herself, Mrs. Alfred Gatty, Mrs. Ewing, and Mrs. Sidney Lear. The palace was also filled daily with clergy and county magnates, discussing diocesan synods and other local affairs with their bishop.

As the fifteen children grew up, there was again created that environment of 'music and metaphysics' which Cardinal Manning remembered after fifty years as having 'quickened his undergraduate wits' when he and Bishop Moberly were at Balliol together. All through the Salisbury days, Miss Yonge remarks on the Moberlys' 'habits of fun, games, and habitual merriment, animation, and playfulness. . . . As long as the palace was their home', she said, 'the family's general characteristics were untouched—full of interest in everything, tender kindness, cheerfulness, and keen bright wit as brilliant as ever.'

Those large Victorian families were a world in themselves, and when their members went outside they felt almost as if they were among people who spoke an alien tongue. Most houses simply had not got room for more than the families themselves, and this tended to make their occupants more than ever self-sufficient. The fifteen Moberlys made an immense society, with common interests, common tastes, and common memories. Careers which had been begun in the palace were continued outside, and were closely followed with a sense of proprietorship by the family at home. Married daughters transplanted cuttings of the family tree to found new plantations elsewhere. This gradually widening community had shared common successes in the past, anticipated common prospects in the future, and enjoyed a common stock of jokes. The small families of the present day have ended all that, though that many-sided spontaneous culture must anyhow have gone, in these days of compulsory universal education. Those people wore their learning lightly, taking it for granted. They did not know the word 'highbrow'.

The Moberlys found a most congenial atmosphere in the close of Salisbury, filled, as it was, with cultured and artistic canons and their ladies; and the newcomers soon added to its reputation by giving the city the name of being the most musical place in England. The family alone could produce two simultaneous string quartets; they sang much choral music: they played the piano: one of the brothers founded and conducted a Musical Society which comprised most of the amateurs living in the Test and Avon valleys.

It must be remembered that in the England of Queen Victoria no family was a commonwealth. A father was an absolute monarch, even when he did not chance to have the blood of a race of tsars flowing in his veins, and Bishop Moberly was not only a tsar's descendant. He had been the headmaster of Winchester. His children were afraid of him. Although he was kind to them, 'walking and joking with the elder boys and girls', they never forgot that he was the dreaded schoolmaster.

A family at this time was no haphazard growth. It was regulated according to a clearly conceived pattern. It was a constitutional body, based on law, and every member had his own place in the social scheme under the father, who was the supreme head of all. The Bible and the Roman law provided the code, and these august origins gave it a sacred character. Something like this existed in all families, but a clergyman had to set a special example in fatherhood as in everything else. Severity was a recognized element in Victorian Christianity. Quite in her old age Miss Moberly spoke of the different attitude to evil possessed by people in the twentieth century and in the generation of her father and Mr. Keble. 'People must recognize again', she said, 'that evil must be *fought*, it must be recognized, denounced, and *fought*. The denunciatory passages in the Psalms are the outcome of a very advanced spirituality. I am convinced of this. The shallow thought of this generation does not see it. I learnt this from my father and Mr. Keble. The dislike of the denunciatory Psalms comes from the irreligous idea that death is the worst evil that can happen to a man.'

She went on to say that 'Mr. Keble was tender, kind, very stern, and very self-disciplined. We were much afraid of him. He had such a very high standard.'

Severity, obedience, and fear were all approved in the palace at Salisbury, and Annie Moberly was brought up to accept them as essentials in the training of character. Though she admired and appreciated him from childhood, she felt, as all his family did, that her father was 'so much above us' that she was always afraid of him, till she found herself taking care of him in his last illness.

Few people are now frightened of their parents, and this genera-tion looks upon it as a completely wrong attitude. Yet Annie Moberly's remarkable character was developed in this now depre-cated atmosphere.

The family was then not only the foundation unit of society with laws as clearly codified as the wider organizations that have grown out of it; it was also the school for learning the art of living. Win-chester had taught the Moberlys that 'Manners makyth man' and the different generations could then be on easy terms, in spite of the formality of their manners. That formality was part of the art of living, which lays down rules for the family among other social relationships. To-day there is no art of living. Nature is the ideal. The convention then was that the intercourse between parents and children should be expressed in the language of the parents. Nowa-days parents adopt the speech of their children. This does not neces-sarily mean that they are nearer each other.

Mrs. Moberly with her recollections of her Italian girlhood made a new thing of the old Winchester motto. There were a great many parties at the palace, all carefully planned and thought out. Enor-mous parties for diocesan conferences when clergy from remote villages met, as their fellow guests, neighbouring parsons probably living only ten or twelve miles away from themselves, and yet complete strangers. Learned parties for translators of the Bible; musical parties for friends of the brothers; friendly parties for a few intimates from the close; and family parties for all ages. Annie Moberly's social training was a very varied thing.

And what did they make of her, these twenty years in the palace at Salisbury? Well, grafted on to her inborn nature they made her what she was; but she did not find life too easy during those years at Salisbury. She was rather a lonely one in the family. Six sisters had come before her, and three brothers, and these made the elders of the party. She wandered dreaming about the garden, telling no-one her thoughts. Hours were spent at the piano, and she gave herself a liberal education, browsing freely in her father's library. She was not content with the books of the day, and she taught herself to read both Greek and Hebrew because she could never be satisfied by reading the Bible only in translation. There were no examinations for her to pass and she never thought of such a thing. Unconsciously she was training herself for the university career which she then so little knew was awaiting her. She did this by simply following her own bent, and her bent happened to be books and music. And possibly because there was then no organized system for the higher education of women, the women who cared for things of the mind were often more cultured than the women of to-day. Their reading was individual. Their minds became like the old family still-rooms in which could be found rare home-made preserves, curious wines, and essences subtly distilled; instead of resembling the standardized contents of the tins which are now displayed in the windows of multiple shops.

People sometimes speak as if the women of pre-university days were complete ignoramuses; and yet, from among them, there came the first heads of women's university colleges—women whose minds were stored with the learning of the past, who had the business capacity to found colleges without any tradition behind them, and who possessed the statesmanlike qualities enabling them to lead their sex into the age-old, conservative academic world. The first women's colleges could not find their Heads in the ranks of those who had gained the school certificate, for those ranks did not exist. They therefore looked among women who had grown up in the world of public service, the daughters and sisters of statesmen and bishops. Cambridge chose a daughter of Mr. Gladstone and a sister of Mr. Arthur Balfour; among Oxford's first choices were the daughters of the Bishops of Lincoln and Salisbury.

During the last year of her father's life, when he was very weak and failing, Annie often used to push him in a chair to his meetings and services and he sometimes seemed sad and depressed about the future of his family. 'What will do you when I am gone?' he used to say. 'You will be very poor.'

Then she gaily answered, 'Oh, I shall find work.'

She found that this cheered him, though she could not think what she would be able to do. Teaching was the only profession for a lady and she knew she would make a very bad governess. She used to say to herself, 'If I go on saying this, I shall have to mean it', and yet she saw no way out.

When the Bishop was evidently nearing his end, Annie one day walked out into the garden and sat beneath a chestnut-tree, playing idly with some green chestnuts which had fallen to the ground. As she played with them, she found that she was praying and her prayer was something like this:

'Never mind what happens to *me*, only let it be easy for *him*.'

She felt that she had made a vow to God, and when (contrary to what the doctor expected) her father's death came quickly and peacefully, she felt that she was obliged to keep that vow. She must go where she was sent.

Before the next bishop took possession, there were some months of rather difficult life at the palace, and then Annie went once more to the seat under the chestnut-tree. The family was on the point of leaving, the chestnuts were still there, now grown brown and ripe. She could not see into the future, yet her vow rose up before her, and she could not tell how she could keep it. There was no choice before her. Then she felt a hand on her head, and, close beside her, a bright clear voice said:

'*Better than you think.*'

She was so startled that she got up and went indoors; and then came an unexpected letter from Miss Wordsworth, asking her to come to Oxford and take charge of Saint Hugh's, the projected new hall for women students. It seemed to point to a vocation. It felt like a call, and the memory of this often helped her when she was unhappy in those early days.

People who only knew Miss Moberly by reading her famous *Adventure at Trianon* will say here:

'Of course she expected a ghostly voice. It was like her.'

But nothing could have been less like what would have been expected that afternoon by the bishop's daughter in the palace garden at Salisbury. In the severely spiritual atmosphere in which she had grown up, there was a rigid disapproval of any form of spiritualism. She shared this disapproval. She believed that such practices were wrong, and were discountenanced by the Church. All through her life, she disliked speaking of any experiences of her own in this direction, and she never did so except in the presence of people whom she trusted and who shared her Christian faith. A characteristic memory of Annie Moberly is the blank snubbing look which came over her face when a stranger tried to sound her on these subjects. The conversation fell dead.

While there is no doubt that she did possess unusual powers, she never attempted either to cultivate or to develop them. Such an idea was anathema. Anything of the kind was a free gift from God, to be accepted without human interference as to the manner of its giving. To such an experience she applied Saint John's test: 'Beloved, believe not every spirit, but try the spirits, whether they are of God.' She had been known to say that spiritualistic séances drove the spirit out and let the devil in. She often recalled the warning given by the anonymous English mystic of the fourteenth century in *The Cloud of Unknowing*:

'Ofttimes the Devil feigneth quaint sounds in their ears, quaint lights and shinings in their eyes, and wonderful smells in their noses: and all is but falsehood.'

She never spoke of more than two or three things in her life which might come under the head of 'quaint sounds or lights or shinings', and then she applied the medieval test. She asked whether the visions had helped or hindered her in devotion to God, humility, or other virtues. She was like Joan of Arc in the simple, matter-of-fact way in which she responded to her voices when they came. The voice under the chestnut-tree was one of these experiences.

An earlier one is even more remarkable, for it happened when she was quite a little child, and its effect was indeed to give her, throughout her life, a heavenly view of this world.

She was about five or six and was walking hand in hand with her nurse on Saint Catharine's Hill outside Winchester.

'I must have been very small,' she said, 'for I remember the pressure of my nurse's thumb as she held my hand. Then suddenly I saw Winchester with its towers and spires enlarged in a wonderful way. It was as if it was inside some greater place right up against the sky—most wonderful and glorious. And as I looked, I heard a voice say *two words*—words I had never heard, and certainly couldn't have spelt:

'PINNACLED REALITY.

'I told no-one. Children don't. But I have never forgotten it, and I have often expected to come across those words in my reading of poetry, or in other literature, but I never have.'

Nearly forty years passed between the hearing of these two voices, years which were passed in the manner which I have described, living a very disciplined life under the domination of a schoolmaster bishop, and yet a life nearly always in a crowd—a crowd composed of the family, of ecclesiastics, of learned people, and of amateurs in music and the arts. But during the last months at the palace two other experiences have been recorded which show that at this period Annie Moberly was especially sensitive to visions of the kind which are now associated with her name. The first was a week before her father died when she was going with one of her sisters to tea with some friends in the close. As they were leaving the palace garden, its great gates were thrown open, and two men carrying a coffin passed them, apparently on their way to the palace.

'At the time it did not seem unnatural,' said Miss Moberly. 'Things never do'; but they did wonder about it, as no-one had died in the immediate neighbourhood. They spoke about it to the Misses Vaux with whom they were going to tea. These ladies immediately wrote it down and when the bishop died a week later they showed what they had written.

The story of 'The Bishops' Birds' is now well known. Annie Moberly's connection with it is that an hour or two after her father's death she walked alone into the palace garden, and there

C

saw two great white birds which rose from the ground before her. The spread of their wings was immense, and their feathers were dazzlingly white. They were unlike any birds she had ever seen, and she watched them fly over the cathedral and disappear towards the west. That evening she described them to one of her elder brothers, and he said that there was a quite well authenticated tradition that birds like these had been known to appear at the death of a Bishop of Salisbury. That phrase, 'quite well authenticated' is typical of Annie Moberly. At that particular time she must have had too much on her mind to seek for evidence as to the appearances of these birds in the past; but she did not forget it and by degrees she collected all the stories which had come down from the previous century. Years later, when she was on a holiday in Constance, she remembered that Bishop Hallam of Salisbury had died there during the Council of Constance, which took place in 1414. With her passion for research she hastened to the *Mairie* and examined the town records. After much search through the ancient documents she found the account of the dead bishop lying in state in the great hall of the town. There followed these words: 'then came the great sign of the birds'.

It was a wonderful moment for her and she seemed to have found the original source of the legend of the Salisbury bishops' birds. The record said that a great flock of strange birds had then alighted on the roof of the hall where they stayed all night making harsh discordant cries. At morning, they vanished.

Further researches into recorded appearances of these birds do not come into this story of a Victorian lady of Wiltshire, but what does come into it is that this Victorian lady first of all believed her own eyes and then tried, by careful historical research, to verify what those eyes had seen. She may have been the seventh daughter of a seventh child, but that sort of thing carried no weight with the daughter of a bishop of Salisbury who had also been the headmaster of Winchester.

The Miss Wordsworth who invited Annie Moberly to take charge of Saint Hugh's Hall was herself the Principal of Lady Margaret Hall at Oxford. She was the daughter of a Bishop of Lincoln, and her brother was to succeed Bishop Moberly at Salisbury. These bishops belonged to a learned and intellectual group,

Miss Annie Moberly

and in making her appointment, Miss Wordsworth already knew the milieu from which she had chosen her nominee. She knew Annie to be the daughter of a former fellow and tutor of Balliol and of a headmaster of Winchester. She was well acquainted with the severely spiritual atmosphere of John Keble and Charlotte Yonge. If she looked back a generation or two, she could see on all sides consuls whose descendant was bound to possess some business capacity.

Probably she did not look back so far as Peter the Great, or know that he had any claim to be in the picture. So she did not guess that within the chrysalis, whose outer skin had been formed by the Anglican Church, was a winged creature instinct with Slavonic mysticism, with, flowing in her veins, the blood of a race whose Church was built, not on the rock of Saint Peter, but on the transcendental personality of Santa Sophia, the Divine Wisdom. For a Russian there is nothing strange in seeing visions. Annie had seen 'Pinnacled Reality' as a little child: she had met a coffin at the palace gates: but she did not think these experiences were anything to boast of. If she did not speak of them when she was being chosen for her new post, it was because she knew that the qualities desired in her were those which she liked to believe that she shared with Miss Wordsworth, and not those peculiar to herself.

The first Saint Hugh's was not in appearance like either the ancient colleges of Oxford or Cambridge, or the well-designed, but less imposing modern buildings which now house the women undergraduates. It was frankly a north Oxford lodging house—one of those suburban villas in which the university dons had found refuge when the law of celibacy was abandoned for their convenience, and they exchanged the snugness of common rooms and college lodgings for the comforts of Victorian home life. For a woman whose taste had been formed in Winchester and in Salisbury Close, there was nothing architecturally inspiring in 24 Norham Road. Nor was there anything typically collegiate in the groups of seven or eight students who assembled in the commonplace little house. The principal had to create all that. At this moment, she felt it was a disadvantage that she did not even possess what in those days would have passed for a 'regular education'; and she now felt very shy and diffident, clinging to the fact that she was at any rate a 'loyal Oxford person' because of her father's connection with Balliol, and she said 'the best part of me was that I came from a big public school'. Life with her father had impressed upon her the fundamental importance of loyalty, discipline, self-control, and what she called balanced common sense. This had been deliberately taught her by men trained in the Oxford Movement, which she always said was spiritually founded very deeply on common sense, discipline, and mental culture. Anything founded on mere enthusiasm was repudiated by its leaders. In this it sounds unexpectedly like the eighteenth century.

Near the end of her life Annie Moberly said of her appointment to Saint Hugh's, 'I never for a moment thought myself the right person in the right place. My hope was that if good manners, good temper, and good sense did not fail, I should be helped to pull through. I liked girls, and could generally get on well with them, but I could not pose as superior in mind or purpose to anyone. My ruling principle was to be entirely *myself*: the strain of trying to be anything more would have broken me down. There were tempestuously effective people on the council and in the world, with whom I could not compete. I just went on.'

So this Victorian lady was transplanted from Wiltshire to north Oxford, and she proceeded to organize her life at Saint Hugh's Hall as nearly as possible as it would have been organized at the Hall, Salisbury—the house into which the bishop's family moved when they left the palace. Perhaps it was all rather too ladylike, but that was not really a disadvantage. The other side was bound to come in sooner or later, and it was probably a good thing that the traditions of this traditionless little college should be first created by one who valued the old-fashioned feminine modes of living. Actually Annie remained at Saint Hugh's for twenty-nine years, so her policy had time to take root.

Evening parties were in the tradition which she carried with her from Salisbury; and the Saint Hugh's ones were held in Miss Moberly's own drawing-room, which was indeed the only room in the house big enough for entertaining. Tea and coffee, music and conversation, were the entertainments provided, and this was also the Oxford idea of parties. But Annie remembered the unwieldy diocesan parties at Salisbury, in days when many of the clerics from

MISS ANNIE MOBERLY
from the crayon portrait by Leslie Brooke in the possession of
St. Hugh's College

BARBARA TOWNSEND IN HER EARLY TWENTIES
from a painting by Alfred Weigall; background (unfinished) by
Rex Whistler

remote parishes in Wilts and Dorset were almost as untravelled as their flocks. To cross the floor of the great drawing-room at the palace seemed, to one of these unsophisticated clergymen, more alarming than it would have been to cross the ocean on the way to becoming a missionary. So, once a guest had found a chair, he was often stuck for the evening. He dared not move. Mrs. Moberly had taught her daughters to watch for this possible constipation, and to check it. So nothing seemed to Annie more essential for the success of a party than to stop any attempt at conversation *à deux*. The students learnt to be sheep dogs, feverishly hustling their flocks from one fold to another.

Music was quite another thing. The string or vocal quartets conducted by the principal would anyhow have kept the guests quiet, and the students were expected to encourage this.

Annie Moberly's day was modelled on the day of a hostess in any moderately sized house of the period. She began by 'doing the housekeeping'. Not very well, it must be admitted; for though in theory she believed that all women should possess the domestic virtues, in real life they bored her, and she had no interest in the preparation of food. In this she belonged to her generation, for mid-Victorian ladies were accustomed to plenty of servants, and had not been, like their grandmothers, brought up in the stillroom.

Moreover, Saint Hugh's was understaffed, and the students made their own beds, boiled their kettles, filled their hot-water bottles, and washed up their tea cups. Miss Moberly naturally did none of these things. She hardly realized that anyone else did them.

Having ordered the meals, or, rather, having arranged that the old cook should cook whatever she thought best, Annie generally found that she had some shopping to do in the town. After this, she returned to her sitting-room, and spent the greater part of the day in it, reading Greek and Hebrew, as well as the histories of the first fifteen centuries of the Christian era. The room was furnished with heavy mid-Victorian 'pieces'; from the palace at Salisbury: portraits of her mother and grandmother hung on the wall, to suggest to the ethnologist that the unexpected variety of elements in Annie Moberly's nature was exactly what should have been expected in any one of such strangely mixed blood. But the theological books on the shelves, coming from the bishop's library, looked heavy enough to have weighed down any eccentricities of character. They didn't do this, though they contributed towards making her very alarming on first acquaintance, especially for newly arrived students whose highest idea of education hitherto had been the sixth form of a provincial high school.

As we know, severity, obedience, and fear were all considered at the palace at Salisbury to be healthy elements in the training of youth, so Annie would not have cared had she been told that most of her students were rather afraid of her.

'Why should they be?' she might have asked; but the fact that they were, would not have distressed her.

When a student mastered her instinctive nervousness enough to allow her to tap on the door of the principal's room, and to put her head round it, Miss Moberly rather conspicuously put down the weighty tome she was perusing and welcomed the visitor with her peculiarly brilliant smile. She could, and did, give very good advice, and the girl who had been brave enough to tap on the door and to make that first plunge nearly always found her courage rewarded.

Saint Hugh's at one time had among its students a little group of Russian aristocrats, whose 'wardrobe rooms' stocked with wonderful furs and expensive dresses, as well as their attendant 'governesses', gave them some prestige in the eyes of the ordinary students. At one time this foreign element began to practise spiritualism, 'calling up' famous historical characters, and frightening their neighbours in their corridor with stories of spooks. This was the kind of thing which Annie thought very wrong, and as soon as she heard what was going on she sharply put her foot down. But she administered neither an ecclesiastic nor an academic reproof. She did not flatter the culprits by suggesting that they, with their ridiculous tappings and table-turnings, could have the smallest effect on the world of spirits. She acted dynastically. The descendant of Peter the Great rose to the situation.

She sent for the young Russian ladies, and in her most matter-of-fact manner she spoke:

'What do I hear? It is outrageous that three unimportant young women, who nevertheless are the daughters of courtiers of the Tsar, and so might be expected to know something of court etiquette, should have the impertinence to imagine that they could summon into their presence Anne of Austria, Queen of France. In life she might or she might not have permitted you to be presented to her. She certainly would not have done so had she been informed of anything of this kind.'

That was all. Miss Moberly succeeded in making these pseudo-spiritualists feel as foolish as she thought them.

There were two of Annie's Oxford activities in which she found it more or less easy to behave like the principal of a college—her musical societies and her Sunday Bible classes. She came from a family which really was a musical society in itself and the little community at Saint Hugh's could produce music on much the same scale. Musical girls were naturally attracted to the Hall, and they were quickly formed into quartets, orchestras, and madrigal societies, meeting in her sitting-room on several evenings in the week. She was always closest to the students who belonged to these societies. They really were her friends.

Then there were the Sunday evening divinity lectures in the principal's room after dinner on Sundays. Here she revealed her mind as she did nowhere else. Her course on the Apocalypse of Saint John was subsequently published as *Five Visions of the Revelation*, but the printed page completely fails to reproduce the impression given during those evenings in the sitting-room. The girls were grouped about on sofas, chairs, and cushions; and the one light in the room stood beside Annie, shining on her handful of manuscript, her Bible, her pile of reference books, and her pale animated face. But it was not the lamp that illuminated her. It was the Revelation of Saint John. She altogether forgot her surroundings, as in the quick utterances of her odd cracked voice she conjured up before her hearers the Golden City, its walls blazing with multi-coloured jewels, the seven lamps burning everlastingly, the strange heraldic beasts who worship before the throne, the clash of warfare in Heaven, when the dragon was hurled down into hell, the woman clothed with the sun, crowned with the stars and with the moon under her feet, and the great multitude which no man could number. As she herself was carried away by the wonders of these visions, she swept her hearers into her confidence. She spoke through a silence vibrating with her own emotion. And none of this appears in her book. That too was typical of her. A book was a book. A commentary was a commentary. Who was Annie Moberly to presume to change the standard type of such works as laid down by the S.P.C.K. in the early days after the Oxford Movement? She could not altogether control the coruscations of her imagination when it was set on fire in the semi-darkened room of hers in Oxford; but an orthodox Anglican commentary must not go outside the ordered progression of the faith as it had come down from apostolic times to the nineteenth century.

In her writings, Annie Moberly always played for safety. She never wanted to shock people, to startle them, or to make them talk, either about herself or her subject. She was honestly distressed at the sensation made a few years later by her account of her visit to Trianon. She did her best to make that into a dull book, stressing only the historical aspect of her experience, and merely trying to prove that the details were 'well authenticated'. But it was too good a story to be buried under heaps of research, however carefully the writer had combed through their details. Although she believed that she had left nothing to arouse controversy, the world went mad over 'the best ghost story of the day'. It had, however, been published anonymously, so that Annie could continue to assume complete ignorance of the subject if ever it was raised in her presence.

This attitude of caution was probably natural to all well-brought-up Victorian ladies. It was contrary to their every instinct to descend into the arena of controversy; but in Annie Moberly's case, the reserve, characteristic of her date, was accentuated by the way her family had handled her first book. *Dulce Domum* is a very delightful and original history of Bishop Moberly, his family, and their homes, although its first draft was infinitely more delightful and original than the published version. The family insisted upon cuts, and the auther was too well disciplined to gainsay them, though she very much felt their criticism. Long afterwards, looking back upon that book, and knowing what she could have made of it, if she had been given a free hand, she said, 'they made me take out one thing after another, which they thought too familiar. They did not trust me. They might have done so. I had very good taste, but they did not believe it!'

I shall not here relate the story of Annie Moberly's Trianon visit, as it is already well known and can easily be read in her own account of it—*An Adventure*. The way that book is written, and the author's whole treatment of the experience, reveal much about her character. Her actual manner of telling the story shows her meticulous powers of observation. Every detail is noticed with a precision very unlike what one would expect from a 'visionary'. It is quite short, and it is not 'written up' with any literary grace. Rather it is jotted down in the style in which a policeman might make notes in his pocket book. Far the larger part of the book is given to an analysis of the 'well authenticated' facts bearing upon the scenes and events in the vision itself. That is what always interested her—the historical background.

There exist several other stories of Annie Moberly's second sight which are less generally known. It is difficult to record these now that she has been dead some years, because she would not consider an account written after so long to be 'well authenticated'. She always asked for first-hand evidence; yet she was so reserved about her own experiences that it is difficult now to find anyone who had heard her tell her stories, and who can aver that the version they give you was written down at the time, from her own lips.

One I can tell here, as she herself told it to me more than once, and I have also received a written account of it from a member of her own family. This account corresponds, almost word for word, with my own recollection.

Annie Moberly was in Paris about a year before the outbreak of the 1914 war, and one day she visited the picture galleries at the Louvre—always a favourite haunt of hers. She said:

'*As we came down the great staircase, we saw the usual crowd coming along the vestibule below. In it, and very noticeable in it, was a tall, commanding, yet graceful man. He must have been of unusual height, for he equalled the height of a child sitting on its father's shoulder, close by in the crowd. The man had a small golden coronal on his head, and wore a loose toga-like dress of some light colour. I looked at him and he looked at me. Our eyes literally seemed to meet. It was not a face, or a figure, to forget; for his whole bearing was of unusual nobility and gracefulness. He looked from side to side, as though taking it for granted that he was noticed.*'

In this it appeared that he was mistaken, for when Annie asked the name of this remarkable stranger from some officials standing near, none of them had seen him. It was obvious that a man of six or seven feet high could hardly have passed unnoticed, if he really consisted of flesh and blood, and the inference was that he was an apparition. Annie did not let it end there. She resolved to find out, if possible, who this tall, graceful, and proud-looking man could be. At first, his great height made her think of Charlemagne, but she soon found that this was a false scent. The dress was wrong. Continuing to search through books of costume, she discovered that the pattern of the toga, the shape of the coronal, and the rather unusual way in which the straps of the sandals were wound round the leg, all indicated a Roman emperor of the fourth century. Portraits showed that the early ones were all bearded men, and the first to be clean-shaven was Constantine. Could this be her man? More search among portraits and medals revealed that this was the case. Then came the question, why should Constantine be seen in the Louvre? Further research disclosed that the palace was built at a point on the course of a former Roman ceremonial road, leading from the centre of the city to the great camp outside. On two occasions in his career did the Emperor Constantine march in procession down this road.

This was another instance of Annie Moberly's gift of stepping back into the past. Her constant hope was that these experiences would some day be of value to scientists investigating the nature of Time; and it was with this in view that she made careful records of what she saw and also carefully sought for historical authentication of the details of her visions.

Another story of the same kind is even more striking because it is concerned with a person whose very name was unknown to history till Miss Moberly brought it again to the surface. Here is a part of what she wrote at the time about this experience of hers.

'*As I have never seen Cambridge I mean to go there this week. We planned this on Saturday June 21st and yesterday June 23rd, between sleeping and waking in the early morning, I saw a vivid picture of an open space with some buildings, which I called King's College, though I have no doubt that it was entirely unlike the real King's College. On my right hand, there was more or less open ground, ending in a churchyard . . . on the left hand were buildings and a chapel, it stood a little forward from the buildings of which it formed a part.*

Miss Annie Moberly

'We went to this chapel (which was small) and at the door was a man in some sort of dark cassock, who told us that we could go in. A funeral service in Latin was just coming to an end, and I noticed, among the congregation of dark-gowned men, scarlet and purple robes, as well as white surplices. As the service was nearly over, we went outside to see the procession pass . . . first, some acolytes and censer boys came out, then a few clerics, followed by two cardinals (?) in scarlet; one was tall, and had white lace on the skirt and the undress cap. He was pompous and seemed important. The other suggested a university professor; he looked more keen and observant, and moved less pompously.

'The coffin was more square and seemed more ornamented than one sees to-day. There was some coloured painting on it, and on the end where the feet would be was the name:

ARNOLPHUS M——

I could see no more.

'Behind it came some men in dark gowns, and last of all a group of tall thin women in white woolly cassock-like skirts, with dark pointed hoods over their heads. I thought one of them (who had an old face) might have been the mother.

'The procession went from the chapel on the left hand along a road close to the opposite buildings, towards the little churchyard, which sloped considerably away. There were in it some small half-sunken wooden crosses, but it all looked old, with the ground irregular and the grass long . . . afterwards I heard someone say that the second word on the coffin was "Magister".

'Written June 24, 1913.'

On the following day, Annie went to Cambridge, and there of course found that nothing in the buildings of the present King's College suggested the scene of her vision. On her first day in Cambridge, she says that she 'went to see King's College Chapel, and was shown what was called the "Burial Chantry" on the north side of the nave. As this was exactly where the graveyard would have been, I asked whether there had been one in that part and was told that the churchyard of the old church of Saint John Baptist (long disappeared) had reached from the centre of the nave of the present chapel to Clare College on that sloping ground. On account of the slope, the chapel was raised four feet on that side and the chancel seven.

'. . . Neither of our morning's guides, nor the old man at the second-

hand bookshop, knew of any chapel having stood on the south side; but in an old map we saw that before the new large quadrangle was created, there were buildings on the left hand perhaps in connection with a Carmelite monastery which was very near. This makes me wonder whether the "women" were really white friars.

'The Carmelites settled in Cambridge at the beginning of the thirteenth century. In the middle of that century they moved from their first settlement at Newnham to the site indicated on the map, on the southern side of what is now King's College.'

Annie Moberly went to the British Museum to seek information about the Carmelite Superiors during the thirteenth century. There she found the heads of national groups in the Order were called 'Magister', and were under the General of the Order. One English Carmelite who died a General after having been Magister in this country was named Radulphus which is another version of Arnolphus. He was renowned as a very holy man. Celestial lights were seen over his head. His body was sent to England for burial in 1277 but it is not known where it was laid. The Carmelites' habit, regularly black with a white hood, was changed for a time in the latter part of the thirteenth century to be white with a black hood, like the figures in the procession.

Further investigations brought to light certain details about the two ecclesiastics who might have been 'the Cardinals' described by Annie, but this is not the place to analyse this evidence. Enough has been said to indicate her attitude towards such extra-natural phenomena. She was a very modest student and scholar; and, in her own eyes, her one task was so to tabulate the results of her researches that they might in future be of value to scientists and historians.

There was nothing of the journalist about her. Victorian ladies looked on no events in their lives as being possible 'copy'. Whatever Annie Moberly wrote, she wrote remembering that she was the daughter of a scholar and a bishop, and was trained in the school of Charlotte M. Yonge.

MRS.
ALFRED MORRISON

At some time in the first decade of the nineteenth century, a young Army doctor named Robert Chermside was quartered at Blackrock near Dublin, when, on his return home from duty one morning, he had an adventure destined to make considerable changes in the course of his life. He was in the act of letting himself into his house when he heard, coming down the road, the sounds of a runaway horse. In a few moments it had careered madly past him. At the next curve in the road it threw its rider, who lay motionless on the ground, while the noise of the clattering hoofs went on and on, till it was lost in the distance. The doctor ran to the spot where the unconscious stranger lay, and carried him into his own quarters, where he would undoubtedly have died but for the exceptional skill of his rescuer. As it was, he remained in the house for many weeks, recovering slowly.

The injured man was Colonel Wildman of the 10th Hussars, who would, a few years later, purchase Newstead Abbey, notorious then as only lately the home of Lord Byron, and as the scene of many scandalous orgies both real and imaginary. This chance meeting, which can indeed be called 'accidental', was the opening of the long connection of the Chermside family with the home of Byron. Colonel Wildman did not leave young Chermside many more months at Blackrock. He quickly arranged his appointment as doctor to his own regiment, to serve with it both in the Peninsular War and at Waterloo. The two men were lifelong friends.

Years later, when the colonel was an old man living at Newstead, there rode over one day to visit him the little granddaughter of Robert Chermside. She was staying near by, at Papplewick, with Mrs. Walter, her mother's sister; and now Colonel Wildman and his wife fell again under the Chermside charm. They soon invited the little girl to pay them what turned out to be the first of a succession of long visits, and there Mabel used to sit, evening after evening, listening to the colonel's stories of the Napoleonic Wars, in Lord Byron's fantastic refectory hall, the walls of which were now hung with a magnificent set of Gobelin tapestries, brought back by the colonel from the war in Spain. He had been fortunate enough to catch a soldier in the very act of looting these treasures, and with great acumen he had checked this unauthorized act by buying the tapestries from the man who had got possession of them.

More than sixty years later, that little girl had long been Mabel Morrison, and she was often again at Newstead, for her brother Herbert's wife, Miss Geraldine Webb, inherited the place from her father. So it happened that the life of Mabel Morrison, first and last, was associated with the home of the most bizarre of English poets; while in the intermediate years her own home was to be at Fonthill, made famous by William Beckford, a character as eccentric as Byron himself, for she married Alfred Morrison in 1866.

Architecture at Fonthill is catastrophic, and houses there live adventurous lives. The Fonthill House bought by Alfred Morrison's father in 1837 was not the first house on the site. Colt Hoare speaks of three as having existed before the end of the eighteenth century. He calls the first 'Fonthill *antiquus*' and only says of it that it was 'consumed by fire' at an unknown date. Then came 'Fonthill *redivivus*' bought by Alderman Beckford, and also burnt down, in 1755. In this fire perished the alderman's celebrated water organ, which cost £5,000, and which was worked by power from the reservoir on the hill which also supplied the fire pumps. And now, while the water streamed vainly on to the tremendous roaring flames, the while the roof timbers crashed through the burning floors, the organ was heard for the last time to pour forth a torrent of music. Beckford at once built another house, called by Hoare

Mrs. Alfred Morrison

'Fonthill *splendens*'. It cost £240,000, but William Beckford disliked its site, and in 1807 he pulled down all but its laundry wing, a block separated from the main house by a covered colonnade, and it was this comparatively small house, then called the Pavilion, which was bought by Mr. James Morrison.

His son Alfred was then a boy of about sixteen, and at Fonthill they heard Beckford spoken of as quite recently a country neighbour, and as still living at Bath. He had not yet become a tradition. The classical church built by his father was still standing at Fonthill Gifford, and there were old people living who could tell in what spot in the park had been buried the crusaders' coffins which he had removed from the old church. In the family pew were the cushions worked by Beckford's daughter the Duchess of Hamilton, and the rector was the same old clergyman who had shown the church to Lord Nelson on his famous visit to Fonthill in 1800. The workpeople spoke bitterly of Beckford, of his capricious ways and his violent temper. He had treated them like the slaves in his Jamaican plantations, breaking into such a fury when the work on his new waterfall was not carried out to his liking that he turned to and gave the unsatisfactory workman a sound thrashing with his own hands.

William Beckford lived on at Bath till 1844, and about the year 1843, Alfred Morrison walked up one afternoon to the terrace to look at the abbey, a ruin since its great tower fell in upon it in 1825. Another visitor was there before him. An old gentleman, mounted on a sturdy little cob, had halted some way off, and he was gazing at the wood and at the ruins in so absorbed a fashion that he never observed the young man who had come upon him. It was William Beckford. He had ridden over from Bath to look for the last time on all that remained of the most stupendous of all the follies which he and his contemporaries had set upon a hundred hilltops. The old man and the young one looked at it in silence, and then each returned to his own place.

Lord Byron and William Beckford were kindred spirits, and of the same family was Mabel Morrison. It was ordained that the circumstances of her life should lead her from Newstead to Fonthill and then again to Newstead. These places were naturally her homes.

Mrs. Alfred Morrison

The Dr. Chermside who found Colonel Wildman when he had fallen on to his head in the road at Blackrock, and who set him on his feet again, became later on a very famous doctor. He remained with the 10th Hussars till the wars ended with the Battle of Waterloo, and he entered Paris with the Allies; but on the declaration of peace he returned to science, the real interest of his life. He went to Edinburgh to study there in the medical schools. Queen Adelaide made him her doctor, and the king sent him to attend Mrs. Fitzherbert in her last illness. Lord Yarmouth, afterwards the Lord Hertford of the Wallace Collection, brought him to Paris to attend on his mother, Lady Hertford. There he settled as doctor to the British Embassy. He became Sir Robert Chermside, and he and his wife (a Miss Williams of Herringstone in Dorset) were given a small house adjoining Lord Hertford's own, and this was his home till the end of his life. His son Richard Seymour was the father of Mabel Morrison. He took orders in the Church of England and became one of Dr. Hook's curates at Leeds. Here was born in May 1847 his eldest child Mabel.

Her native place was not destined to affect her after-life, as the Chermsides left Leeds almost immediately for Wilton, where Mr. Chermside had been appointed rector. Mabel's home was to be in Wiltshire for the greater part of her life, but throughout her childhood, Wilton was little more than a background for the Europe which spread itself before her eyes. Her earliest memories were those of playing on the *ciré* parquet floor in her grandparents' house in the Rue Taitbout and her first words were spoken there and in French. After Lady Chermside's death, Mabel lived in Paris with Sir Robert for about two years; and when he went, as he often did, to Boulogne, the little girl travelled there with him, and stayed in the farmhouse belonging to the parents of Mélanie her *bonne*. Here she ran fearlessly in and out of the cowsheds, making friends with the cattle; and here too she first learnt how to run fearlessly into the confidence of simple country people. To the end of her life she maintained this natural easy commerce with farm labourers, and keepers, and hand workers of all kinds. Outwardly she became a very great lady, with always something exotic in her way of entering a drawing-room, in the dramatic movements of her hands, and in the slow sidelong turn of her head when she talked or listened with a look of remote amusement half-hidden in her eyelids. All this was very mannered, and a homely British farmer's wife might be expected to find her very alien. On the contrary, it was completely easy for her to become friends with country men and women, though she first learnt the way to do this, not in Wiltshire, but in Normandy.

Wilton too was by no means the typical English country place of the eighteen-fifties. Wilton House was occupied by Sidney Herbert, afterwards Lord Herbert of Lea, and with his Russian mother (the daughter of Count Simon Woronzow, the Russian Ambassador in London) he had lately built the great Romanesque church which dominated the Chermsides' rectory garden. This building, so curiously unexpected among the downs and water meadows of southern Wiltshire, was another of the exotic things to which Mabel Chermside grew up, and for her its campanile stood as naturally among the poplars as did the spire of Salisbury, seen springing from the rounded contours of the plain.

Throughout her girlhood, Mabel travelled far more than most of her contemporaries. Mr. Chermside was *poitrinaire*, which meant for the family several winter visits to the Riviera, though it was a very different Riviera from the one of to-day. No 'Palace Hotels' had intruded their arrogant heads between the high villages and castles of Provence, and the bright Mediterranean coast. No broad tarmac road vibrated under the engines of high-powered cars racing from casino to casino. Cream-coloured oxen drew loads of produce along farm roads; and in the eighteenth-century villas by the sea there lived old Italian countesses who taught Mabel to collect oddly shaped lemons, and to arrange them in elaborate silver dishes. The country had been little changed since the days of the Romans, and when Mabel visited it in later life, she was horrified to find that America had made of it a new place during her own lifetime.

Her tenth year was spent in Pomerania, where she lived with a family called von Torno. Two memories remained from that. She remembered the huge spring washings of the German women, when they spread their mountains of linen upon the river banks; and there was one unforgettable winter night, when they sat listening to the distant howling of wolves. A sound like nothing else.

Surprisingly enough, Mabel was a terrific tomboy, rollicking

D [49]

about on the downs and in the meadows with her two brothers Walter and Herbert, tumbling headlong from a coracle into the Nadder, the stream which bounds the rectory garden, and climbing the trees for miles round. After she had been dressed for a party, Mabel raced out one afternoon to have one last look at a nest in a very high tree; but when her concerned mother pursued her, too late to prevent the escapade, she found the muslin dress neatly folded up at the foot of the tree, and she looked up to see Mabel at its top in her petticoat.

All her life she loved and studied birds and animals. Her brothers and she once painted the cocks and hens a brilliant magenta, thinking that they must be bored with their dull plumage. And as a child, Mabel was followed everywhere by the pet fawn given to her by the keeper, while she carried on her wrist a tame owl, called 'Fuchsia Buds' because of the funny popping sound which it made. There were wonderful rides on the downs with Mary and Maud Herbert, her chief girl friends; and together they watched Mr. Gladstone cutting down trees in the park, and collected chips as keepsakes. Lord Herbert was a wonderful *raconteur*, and all the children enjoyed his endless stories; and it was through him that they all loved and admired his friend Florence Nightingale.

At sixteen Mabel was a singular and beautiful figure to come upon in a country rectory. All her life she had her own peculiar style of dressing, and already she enjoyed collecting amusing costumes in the various countries she visited. She brought back strange headdresses, shawls, and jewels, to add their foreign flavour to her own lavish movements, to the beauty of her face, and to the brilliancy of her speech. The Chermsides were not rich, but Mabel had always her own splendour.

Thus it was not only her temperament, but the circumstances of her upbringing, which made Mabel Morrison, to the end of her life, something like a bird of paradise in the Wiltshire scene: she was different from the wives of the neighbouring country squires.

That childhood of hers is very long ago; yet now and again there reaches us from it a record of some almost forgotten episode illustrating a characteristic which stayed with her to the end—courage, generosity, or the sense of responsibility. It reads almost too like a story from a *Collection of Moral Tales for Nursery Readers*, when one learns that the beloved doctor of the parish of Wilton was in those days named Dr. Good; yet such I believe was the case. To him came one day the little Mabel Chermside, asking him to pull out a tooth, 'and it must be a double one', she said.

Dr. Good looked into the little girl's mouth, and could see nothing wrong, so he asked her where the pain was.

'There's no pain. I only want it taken out.'

The doctor eventually discovered the truth. One of Mabel's uncles used to give the children a reward for bravery when a tooth was taken out—5s. for a single tooth, 10s. for a double one. And Mabel had overheard her parents saying that they really could not afford the port wine which the doctor continually ordered Mr. Chermside to drink. Mabel had immediately rushed off to the doctor, to find the means of taking her part in meeting the family problem. Perhaps this was the very tooth commemorated in a book found at her death in the Littleden library and inscribed, 'With love from your friend Elizabeth Herbert—the price of a double tooth'.

A few years later there comes a story which, alarming as it sounds, puts the child Mabel into a setting nearer to the fantastic world of her later life. Wilton church is built over a large crypt, part of which was originally planned as a burial place for the Herbert family. Directly the church was finished, some coffins from the family vault in the old churchyard were removed to this new place; and about sixteen years later, when Lord Herbert himself died, his coffin was placed, with the rest, in an open recess at the far end of the crypt. For many months Lady Herbert made it a practice to spend some part of each day praying beside her husband's body; and, in order to make this possible, the crypt was unlocked at a certain hour every morning, and locked at night. Mr. Chermside always did this himself, never leaving it to old Musselwhite the parish clerk. On one occasion, when he and Mrs. Chermside were away from home for a few days, the key was given to Mabel, then aged about sixteen. She did her duty conscientiously till one evening, when she and Herbert had been out fishing together, they stayed out later than the time allowed by the strict old nurse who was left in charge of the children. It was extremely exasperating to Mabel that she, the eldest sister, should be packed off to bed in disgrace before the little ones, and she consequently forgot the crypt. She woke in the middle of the night to remember it. Her honour was at stake, and she crept out of bed and down the dark stairs into the garden. Here it was moonlight, but a moonlight broken by hurrying clouds which threw horrid moving shadows about the dark yews in the churchyard, while little puffs of wind made uncanny little sounds. Mabel ran swiftly to the crypt, shut the door at panic speed, and locked it in one instantaneous movement. When it was shut she realized that in that momentary peep into the darkness she had seen (or thought she had seen) a tiny light in the far corner. Was it possible that she had locked someone in among the coffins? Many years afterwards, Mabel Morrison said that in all her life she had never again done so brave a thing as when she went back to that horrible door, unlocked it, and called into the darkness, 'Is there anybody there?' The mere fact that no answer came increased the terror which she had scotched, not killed, and now she fled back to the rectory, and scrambled into bed with a heart which throbbed violently for an hour or more.

Mabel was only nineteen when she was married at Saint James's Church, Piccadilly, to Alfred Morrison, a man twenty-five years older than herself; and with this marriage she entered upon a life really adapted to her remarkable character. Till then she had not found herself. There warred in her the tomboy, the scholar, the artist, and the princely giver; and now from these incongruous elements in the child Mabel Chermside, was to be created the striking and unforgettable personality that was Mabel Morrison. Her husband now owned Fonthill, and he was a very rich man. He was also a man of immense taste and knowledge; and together these two now proceeded, in the place where Beckford had once surrounded himself with his famous treasures, to build up new collections of rare Oriental china and carpets, of pictures, of manuscripts, of lace, of enamels, and many other beautiful objects. And, child as she then was, Mabel, no less than her husband, from the first never contemplated any object for the employment of their wealth other than in such noble and lofty directions.

There were enigmatical currents in the deep channel of her spirit. What was in her mind when her brother Walter found her in her room just before her wedding, seated in her bridal robes, gravely

STILL SKETCHING AT THE AGE OF NINETY-ONE
from a photograph of Miss Townsend by Colonel W. E. Davies, C.M.G., C.B.E., D.S.O.,
late Rifle Brigade

MABEL MORRISON
enamel portrait by Lepec in its contemporary frame

reading the burial service? Certainly this was no commonplace bride, and yet, as certainly, this was no pose, for throughout her life no-one was ever less of a *poseuse*. This will be denied by people who only knew Mabel Morrison by seeing the magnificent sweep with which she entered a room, who watched from a distance her elaborate gestures, or who listened, without really knowing her, to her richly stored conversation. Stupid people who only knew her slightly often thought it impossible that she could be really natural when she was so unlike themselves. Yet, for those who knew her well, if there was in her one quality which never failed, it was her sincerity. When she discarded convention, as she often did, it was from no wish to make an effect; it was because her clear eyes were fixed on the thing within—life and naked truth, which alone interested her. Her grand manner was never a mannerism. It clothed a true grandeur of spirit. And the more closely one knew her, the more one realized the innate candour of her soul.

The tomboy did not die on Mabel's wedding day. It was not his funeral service which she was reading. He reared his head at least once again. The bride and bridegroom had returned from their honeymoon to Basildon, the family house on the Thames, and here Mabel was expected to play her part as the correct matron of the period. But she could not long remain in any mould fashioned for her by other people: she must make and break her own as she pleased. Now there happened to be staying in the house a niece of her husband's who was only three years younger than herself, but who, not yet being 'out', was still permitted by the etiquette of the day to enjoy now and again a little decorous romping. It tells much of the code of manners to which young people were then expected to conform, that it was never forgotten in the family that Mabel Morrison, then a married woman, was known to have thrown the train of her velvet dress over her arm, in order to jump over the flower beds with her sixteen-year-old niece. What made it worse was that the naughty girls were said to have got up at six in the morning to carry out this indelicacy, although the additional touch of the velvet train throws doubt upon this added audacity.

In the first eight years of her married life, Mabel Morrison had five children—the first of these, little Rachel, only living for ten months. Sixty years later, that child still lived vividly in her heart, and she spoke with loving pride of the unsullied spirit for which she had provided a brief lodging, and which had returned to God, its purity unstained. She never looked upon this transient life as having been a futility; it remained for her a wonder.

Five children before she was twenty-seven, and at the same time a very full life of travel, society, slumming (as it was then called), and the immense and varied occupation of making the Fonthill collections which meant constant interviews with experts speaking every possible language—all this made too strenuous a life for any young woman, and for twelve years after the birth of her last child Mabel Morrison made a gallant struggle with suffering. She endured very great pain from an internal illness, and was condemned to be nearly always on her back. She lay in her sitting-room opening upon Carlton House Terrace, and astonished the Londoners by keeping bees outside her window. To watch them was an unfailing amusement. Her children were constantly with her, and she read aloud to them the books of the period—Lilian's *Golden Hours*, Scott's novels, *Dr. Jekyll and Mr. Hyde*, and many French books. Memories remain of New Year's Eves at Fonthill or in London, when the children were allowed to stay up with her till the bells of Hindon Church or of Westminster Abbey told them that the New Year had come in.

During these invalid years, Mr. Morrison built a wooden house on the downs under Great Ridge Wood, commanding a wonderful view southward to the Dorset downs which sweep to the sea. Here Mabel Morrison and her children spent many summer weeks. They only took one servant with them, Mabel's personal maid, but Alfred True the woodman kept guard in the kitchen all night, companioned by his dog. At eight-thirty every morning a dog-cart appeared, containing a housemaid and a kitchenmaid surrounded by hampers of food for the day; and at eleven o'clock a mounted groom galloped up with the post. The children's ponies arrived late in the afternoon, to be petted and fed, and then after tea to be ridden about the downs. By evening all these visitors from the outside world had vanished again: the children had gone to bed, and the everlasting silence of the downs lay round the house. Then Mabel Morrison lay in the veranda, reading some of the great pile of books which arrived for her every day wherever she was; if she was well enough, she sauntered in the wood, or she drove on the downs in the moonlight, watching the glowworms faintly shining in the grass, and the stars blazing away in the enormous circle of the sky. She refused to give in to being an invalid; and when a particularly severe bout of pain had driven her to bed for several days, she insisted upon walking a few steps in the very first hour that she felt better, and on forcing herself to walk a little further each day.

One effect of these years of ill-health was a lasting indifference to conventional hours. Mabel Morrison made it a rule to rest when she felt tired, and never to appear among her family and friends till she was able to take her part in life. So to the end she was only seen at her best, though at what strange hours! At any time in the neighbourhood of midnight she would summon a son, a daughter, or a friend to her side. She had been invisible all day; but now she was well and felt at her most brilliant, so she sat up in bed, put on some unusual but very becoming headdress, and received! The guest often arrived extremely sleepy, having lived a normal life during the day, and now being ready for bed; but all wish for sleep was swiftly banished under the stimulus of these exciting talks. Whatever might be expected of her, Mabel Morrison never failed in being quite unexpected, and especially so in the small hours of the morning. With audacious dash, she leapt from subject to subject. By turns she would be challenging, teasing, or entertaining. Suddenly she would turn upon her companion with a quick direct question on some completely unforeseen subject; and then it was no use pretending to know what one didn't know, to understand what one didn't understand, or to enjoy what one didn't enjoy. Mabel Morrison had a witch's gift for reading one's inmost thoughts, and no acting was good enough to deceive her. She always found one out, and then she would bully and tease and ridicule, when all the while she was opening one's eyes to the real range of the question under discussion, and to the great distances which her own mind had travelled.

At last one reeled back to bed, physically exhausted perhaps, but with the mind whirling with new ideas, the vision widened to un-dreamt-of possibilities, and the wits battered by the swift spring of that elastic mind, which could always come back with a repartee. Then Mabel Morrison was left alone with the mysterious little supper which always waited under silver covers by her bedside, but which often remained untouched till morning.

By the eighties of last century, Mabel Morrison was no longer the invalid she had been for some years, though she did not abandon her privilege of living her own life at her own hours. Hers was one of the first English houses to introduce the French custom of breakfast in bed. It is now general here, and Mabel had been used to it in France from her childhood; but in those days it shocked the Wiltshire neighbours, who looked upon it as immorally indolent. Indolence, however, was never Mabel Morrison's failing. Her life was always immensely full. At Carlton House Terrace and at Fonthill, she entertained most of the distinguished people of the day. In her circle were, among others, George Eliot, Jenny Lind, Leighton, Alma Tadema, the Hubert Parrys, Christine Nillson, Norma Neruda, Robert Browning (a constant dinner guest), Holman Hunt, Woolner, Louisa Lady Ashburton, Lady Marion Alford, the Percy Wyndhams, Lord and Lady Wolseley, and a host more. Mabel's brother Herbert was now a man of great influence in the Near East, and she enjoyed receiving his friends when they came to England, and also choosing richly engraved swords from Wilkinson's for him to present to beys and effendis. Rudyard Kipling and his family were country neighbours, and he named Mabel the Queen of Sheba because of the rare Oriental jewels which she liked to wear; and yet, with that happy chance which so often gave her surprising contacts with days far earlier than her own, she had, too, a link with Shelley through her friendship with Trelawney. Millais painted him as the man in his 'North-West Passage' and the girl in that picture wears the dress worn by Mabel Morrison at the marriage of Hubert Parry and Lady Maud Herbert.

The Morrisons made their great Fonthill collections in the spirit of the eighteenth-century collectors, and indeed they could not do otherwise. They had so many links with the past. Alfred Morrison was born in the year of Napoleon's death, and as a child he learnt French from a woman whose husband had gone to school with Robespierre. Old Mrs. Morrison often told Mabel how she had heard the sailors sob at the funeral of Lord Nelson, and, too, how she had seen Louis XVIII drive through a violent thunderstorm into the gates of the Tuileries on the very day before his death, and he was the brother of Louis XVI. If Mabel Morrison was born too late to possess these direct links with the legendary past which lay behind the Battle of Waterloo, yet she too had played as a baby among the rare treasures collected by Lord Hertford, which were then in his house in Paris, and now form the Wallace Collection. There she could well learn with what exquisite delicacy the most murderous weapons can be decorated, and she doubtless remembered Lord Hertford's weapons when, many years later, she chose those engraved swords for Sir Herbert's Turkish friends. At Wilton, too, Mabel Chermside had been familiar with the famous treasures collected by successive Earls of Pembroke in the days when collectors were dilettanti and not dealers.

The new Fonthill collections soon overflowed the house, then still only the service wing of Alderman Beckford's mansion. Mr. Morrison added three galleries, ugly rooms, but apt for their purpose, which was to display the collections under a top light. The windowless walls gave the rooms a peculiar subterranean character. The marble staircase was carpeted with leopard skins, and the magnificent Oriental china was given a Crystal Palace-like room opening on to the garden. The Morrisons bought not only antiques: they considered that a rich collector should encourage contemporary art, so they welcomed to their house, lacemakers, painters, enamelists, and embroidresses, whose work they bought and whose designs they criticized, perhaps not always in accord with the taste of to-day. But can we be certain that this will for ever be recognized as infallible?

The Morrison collection of autographs has long been dispersed, but during the seventies and eighties of the last century there was formed at Fonthill one of the most remarkable collections of historical documents ever made in this country. In buying these manuscripts Mr. Morrison was no doubt actuated by the true collector's zest in the pursuit of the rare thing for rarity's sake. His wife shared this taste. But the autographs also satisfied what was always her desire in reading any book at all. She desired to get down to the subject rather than to linger over any point of view. She read as a student, seeking the matter rather than the manner. Every true historian thirsts to get back to 'the sources'; but in Queen

Mrs. Alfred Morrison

Victoria's day this was far less possible than it is to-day. Mrs. Morrison possessed the taste for historical research, and in her own house she had the means of gratifying it, in more than one direction.

To take only one instance, Alfred Morrison possessed practically the whole of the Hamilton and Nelson papers, and the mind of his wife was saturated, literally at first hand, with the story of the relations between Lord Nelson, Charles Greville, and Sir William and Lady Hamilton. That story has been told again and again from many points of view. Mrs. Morrison studied it from no point of view at all: she was too near to it for that. She had heard the authentic voice of each protagonist.

Most of the letters came directly from the papers of Charles Greville himself, and his papers included those of his uncle Sir William Hamilton. Others were from the Pettigrew collection compiled for the life of Nelson published in 1849. This correspondence had therefore passed through few hands. It had not been sifted, analysed, or put into shape. It remained the day to day letter bag of four people whose personal relations had become of historical importance because of the positions they held in the world, so the historian in Mrs. Morrison had the rare opportunity of studying this absorbing piece of history from sources till then almost untapped.

The possessor of the actual letters written by Lord Nelson, Sir William and Lady Hamilton, and Charles Greville had no need to study the characters of these people through the eye of any historian or biographer, whether Poet Laureate or lesser fry. Mrs. Morrison had the very words in which they revealed themselves. And she came to the conclusion that the deeper you delve into the self-revelations of men and women in such times of crisis, the more enigmatical they become. Perhaps it was because much of her approach to history came through such unedited sources that Mrs. Morrison's attitude to life was so unprejudiced. This mental attitude led people sometimes to say that she had a mind like a man; but men are not always more free than women from *parti pris*. It was rather that in studying any subject—historical, philosophical, biographical, or religious—her instinct was first of all to strip that subject, as far as possible, from all the trappings concealing it as the result of other people's opinions about it; and to study it in the nude.

The walls of the corridor leading to Mabel Morrison's sitting-room at Fonthill were lined with books, the overflow from the room itself, and most of the volumes were bound in leather bindings designed by herself. She was always a voluminous reader, but what she wanted from a book was less its literary flavour than the matter it contained. She was first and foremost a student, and as far as possible she accepted no knowledge at second-hand. Thus, at a time when it was the fashion to decry the French character as decadent, and to say that the French people had had their day, she refused to accept this verdict on a country she had loved from babyhood. She did more than 'refuse to accept'. She studied the question for herself. For two or three years she set herself to the study of every possible aspect of French life and thought. She read the new French books on politics, philosophy, archaeology, cooking, religion, poetry, criticism, science, art, fiction, military strategy and tactics, and anything else which came to hand. Her ultimate decision was in favour of the French people, and this as the result of no preconceptions on her part. Hers was the unbiased mind of the natural scientist.

And too she had an unfailing memory. All that she read was stored away within easy reach in her brain, and she could call it up with no more difficulty than she would have taken a book from its shelf. She seemed also to have memorized all the pictures in the national collections of France and England at least, and could describe them in detail even when she had not actually seen them for years. She had her own taste in pictures as in all else, and she was not swayed by changes of fashion in art.

At Fonthill they never possessed a very large collection of pictures, but no gallery can be considered negligible which contains some of the choicest of the existing Clouets; and the name of the owner of the Madonna and Child by that anonymous Flemish painter known only as 'the Master of the Morrison Triptych' has an assured place in the history of aesthetics. The small but important group of sixteenth-century French and Flemish pictures was perhaps the peak of Mabel Morrison's appreciation and love of the French. Perhaps her favourite among all was the tragic Clouet of

Mrs. Alfred Morrison

Mary Stuart known as 'Le Deuil Blanc'. She loved it both as an artistic *chef d'œuvre* and also as the poignant likeness of the heroine of one of the most poignant stories in European history. Mrs. Morrison was never an aesthete *pur et simple*. Her mind was built on a foundation of history, and there was generally a touch of the historian in her choice of pictures. She cared for them partly because of their subject. Gibbon the historian as a young man was her most famous Reynolds. She never collected his typical and rather conventional feminine beauties; and the portrait of Madame Geoffrin by François Hubert Drouais was appreciated by her as a picture of one of the most famous Salonières of the eighteenth century.

At Fonthill Mabel Morrison indulged to the full that love for animals which had been one of her chief characteristics as a child. It is regrettable that one of the few things Mr. Morrison ever refused her was her wish to keep an elephant there. It would have been completely in the picture. At one time there were a hundred horses in the stables; and she admired fine creatures of all breeds—horses, Suffolk red polls, and Kellow the bailiff who was the strongest man in Wiltshire. Lord Methuen alone could vie with him in his feat of lifting a cow out of a ditch. There was abundance of dogs always at Fonthill—borzois, dachshunds, chows, exotic Afghan dogs, and a black poodle which Mabel Morrison insisted on putting into a bath of bay rum when he returned once after passing a night or two down a rabbit hole. She carried her bulbul to London, and used to drive with it in Hyde Park.

Mabel's independent mind was an unfailing delight to her husband, in whose eyes she remained the most unique among all the treasures he had collected. He too had his enthusiasms, one of which was an admiration for the local cheeses and cheesemakers. He used to drive a pair of cobs on the downs, with a funny little stunted groom perched up at the back of his phaeton, and he often turned in to the farms to have a talk with the farmers' wives. After one of these expeditions he brought home four or five immense cheeses, which were placed on view on the sideboard in the Tapestry Room, one of the remaining Beckford sitting-rooms, its gilding still decorating the oak panels. Here Mr. Morrison often lunched, his luncheon usually being a second breakfast of coffee and other breakfast dishes, or if he had a guest, there would be priceless old claret

Mrs. Alfred Morrison

brought to the table in its sanded green bottle. The cheeses remained untouched till the family was removing to London, when Mabel suggested taking them with them, or else giving them away. But no. They were too precious, and so they were put away in the safe, to be found there in an over-rotten condition some months later.

Like his wife, Mr. Morrison was a great book-buyer, and his parcels of books, like hers, were delivered almost daily. But unlike her, he was in no hurry to open them, and they remained on the floor in their paper parcels till his wife and daughters insisted on one of their periodical unpackings. Even then, the books were not put away in shelves, as Mr. Morrison said he could see them better on the floor, so there they lay, with a path kept clear between them from the door to his chair. William Morris once said in this room, 'Mr. Morrison is the only man I ever met who keeps his books on the floor and his carpets on the wall'.

At Fonthill, Mabel Morrison's amusing freaks were accepted without question by a rural population which remembered Beckford, though a suddenly improvised display of rockets one night did bring riders from ten miles away, galloping over in the belief that they had seen signals of distress. The people of Islay, who never knew a Beckford, were more pardonably startled when one September night in the early 'nineties they saw great flames roaring to the sky, and apparently coming from Islay House. They crowded to the rescue, to find that a bonfire, thirty feet high, had been suddenly lighted in honour of the birthday of a twelve-year-old guest— Reggie Herbert, now Lord Pembroke.

Mabel's predecessor at Fonthill would have enjoyed the joke as much as she did, when she took her guests one day to a picnic in Great Ridge Wood. Here the ladies made the coffee, while the gentlemen busied themselves in beating up omelettes with their walking-sticks, when the party was disturbed by a sudden outbreak of harsh and stentorian discord. Their hostess had smuggled into the wood the Hindon brass band, which was hidden in the trees very close by, and now, at a signal, from her, it burst forth, with its drums, its cornets, its horns, and its bassoons. The effect was terrific.

Riding habits were then romantic garments, with tight-fitting bodices and long flowing skirts; and, wearing one of these, with on her head a small chimney-pot hat, Mabel Morrison rode a great deal on the downs round Fonthill. She was entirely at home with her grooms, her gardeners, her carpenters, and her sewing women, and her way with them was one of those things in her which was more like the eighteenth century than her own. She had always the presence of the great lady, and yet she could joke and laugh and talk practically of practical things with them on what seemed to be equal terms. One reason was that she always knew very well what she was talking about. It was unfailingly surprising that this seemingly eccentric lady should be one of the most skilful of housekeepers: no cook understood French cooking better than she: every detail in her house was carefully planned and thought out by its mistress. She could talk of hounds with the huntsman as if she were a kennel-man; she planned her gardens with the vision of a le Notre or a Capability Brown. But it was not only this practical common sense which endeared her to her workpeople. There was in her a gaiety and a lightness of spirit which is very rare. She threw herself ardently into life wherever she found it, sailing in the bay at Fishguard; walking on the hills at Islay so untiringly that the old woodman remarked that 'Mistress Morrison is so nimble on her feet'; making friends with *cochers* in the streets of Paris; and always succeeding in getting a laugh out of depressed old gentlemen selling antique books at the bookstalls across the river. She did whatever came into her head, as on one occasion when someone stared at her rather rudely in the train, she put up her parasol and sat behind it.

In the eighties and nineties Mabel Morrison's life was full of colour and variety, surrounded, as she was, by her many friends and those of her children, now growing up. She took a great part, with Princess Christian, Lady Grosvenor, and Mrs. Percy Wyndham, in inaugurating the South Kensington School of Art Needlework; and with Mrs. Lowther she began the Amateur Art Exhibition. Both of these remain to testify to the practical enthusiasm of Mabel Morrison and her friends.

The Fonthill House of Mabel Morrison's day stood among lawns and trees, with the lake before it, and some fine pieces of statuary placed here and there. At Shawford the garden was a topiary one, with, in its centre, the circular old sunk cockpit which she was enchanted to discover there. In neither case were flowers the main feature, and yet her tenderness for flowers was almost as great as if they were human beings. She would never pick one unless she thought it would live longer in water than on the plant; and the few cut flowers which she brought into the house were tended two or three times in the day. She loved talking of flowers, their forms, their habits, and their individual characters. But in gardening, the landscape came first.

Old age was Mrs. Morrison's supreme and ultimate achievement. Most old ladies are deemed to have fulfilled their vocation if they succeed in growing old gracefully. This means that they must find contentment in receding into the background, and becoming with the years an ever fainter shadow of what they were in their prime. They should allow the present to drift remotely by, without interrupting their quiet preoccupation with the past. They should welcome visitors with gentle pleasure, and should be ready, when invited, to relate their early memories, though at not too great a length. Mrs. Morrison did nothing of the sort. She grew old in her own way.

To begin with, there was her appearance. White hair held no terrors for her. She met it with outstretched hands; and for the last twenty-five years of her life she dressed like a French lady of the time of Louis XV, recapturing for herself the beauty and the character of the heaped-up white wig of that period. Her hair was dressed in the fashion of a Gainsborough picture, surmounted often by a great mob cap, while round her head and chin was wound a scarf of lace or of pale pink tulle. This was fastened at the side of the throat, and usually secured by a somewhat enigmatic brooch—a note of interrogation formed of large diamonds. Visitors to Fontwill, to Shawford, or to Littleden often came upon their hostess walking in the garden thus attired, and carrying in her hand one of the many odd walking-sticks which it amused her to collect. But she did not lean upon her stick in the manner expected from old ladies. No. She held it well away with the free gesture of a drum-major wielding his staff; and as she walked in the garden she was often so absorbed in her thoughts that she seemed neither to hear nor to see the approaching guest. Her figure was always erect, but her head was sometimes bent, looking at the ground, or at some flower beside her, and she smiled to herself as if at a secret thought.

She at once swept the new arrival into the swift stream of the ideas that were in her mind, very often by means of those startling questions which had always given her so much pleasure. In putting these questions she sought one of two alternatives. In the first place, she was immensely interested in other people's ideas, and sincerely anxious to learn what they were. She respected the individual point of view, even, and perhaps most of all, in the case of a very unsophisticated person or a child. Failing this, she sought for amusement, in the case of persons possessed of no ideas of their own, but thinking it necessary to improvise an imitation. She delighted in watching the wriggling of someone trying to say what he or she thought was expected. For such insincerity, Mrs. Morrison had no mercy, although as a spectacle it gave her great pleasure; and she greatly enjoyed laying snares for its possessor. It must be admitted that there was a great deal of the tease in this generous, kind-hearted woman; and in the case of anyone she saw to be an intellectual sham, she could be quite pulverizing; while the unhappy person gibbered more and more hopelessly beneath the malicious smile in those bent-down eyes.

After her husband's death, Mrs. Morrison lived for a time at Shawford near Winchester, where she added a wing to the beautiful late seventeenth-century manor house, and was captivated by the rare silver tone of some unstained oak panels which she found there. There was very little of this wood left, and she had more very skilfully pickled to match it, thus anticipating, by her personal fancy, a later and much overworked fashion. But then she had always loved the different woods, respecting in each its individual quality. At Shawford, too, she forestalled the modern vogue for unstained deal, admiring it as the eighteenth-century people admired it when they first saw it, for its reddish colour, and for the harsh strength in its veining, which makes it seem a younger and a more virile wood than the dignified oak.

These bold experiments were typical of Mrs. Morrison. She was ever unaware of passing changes of fashion in taste, were they concerned with dress, with decoration, with art, or with architecture. She chose for herself, with fire, flame, and intuition; but her initiative was rooted in the hard foundation of her clear intellect, and controlled by her wide knowledge. She belonged to the Baroque family—a family who were no parvenus of the seventeenth and eighteenth centuries as some suppose, but who have made their sudden appearances in many different ages. They hail from Babylon, from Imperial Rome, from Constantinople, from Moorish Spain, from Medician Florence, and from the England of Queen Elizabeth. Everywhere they combine a fundamental sense of form with the love of exotic decoration and a taste for the far-fetched. Mrs. Morrison was born with this exciting blood pulsating through her veins, and the course of her life was inevitable.

She liked fine stones, and she usually wore some magnificent pearls, white and black; but she also loved the rich warm colours of the semi-precious stones, and to the end she sometimes wore the exotic jewels which Rudyard Kipling had admired on her, long before. She enjoyed the life history of a yellow Brazilian topaz which had passed through an ordeal by fire, leaving it for ever burning with a flame-like *couleur de rose*. In fact, she was captivated by the elfishness of all the berylline stones which possess an elemental witchery enabling them to play unexpected practical jokes by constantly changing colour. She owned yellow and pale blue sapphires whose kinship could never be guessed with the magnificent deep blue stones of her famous tiara. But most of all she loved the rare Russian alexandrite, which is so persistently tricksy as to make a regular practice of appearing pure green by day and pure red by night. She did not only wear these jewels on her person. She liked to see them herself, so uncut and unmounted stones always lay about on the tables in her room, while imperfect pieces of stained glass charmed her by their unintended colouring. Lumps of coloured glass stood about in places chosen carefully by her where they could best catch and refract the light.

Sitting with her among her rare Chinese furniture, with fantastic gleams lurking in corners where lay the flawed lumps of amber, sphene, and other curious stones, her 'slyness of tongue' (as it has well been called) threw equally unexpected lights on to any subject discussed. She seemed to have forgotten nothing she had ever read in the multitudinous books which lined the walls of every house she inhabited and there were always new and out-of-the-way subjects

E

which at one time or another she appeared to have studied pro-
foundly. Then there would suddenly come from her an impish
remark on nothing in particular, such as 'I sometimes think it must
be the most amazing experience in the world to wake up on the
morning after being made Pope, and to say, I AM INFALLIBLE.'

Mrs. Morrison made a thing true by the power of her will. She
said one evening to a guest at Shawford, 'To-morrow I mean to
have a quiet morning. I shall not come down till teatime. Will you
amuse yourself?'

The guest accordingly sat sewing in the garden hall, when, quite
early in the day, Mrs. Morrison appeared, hastening to and fro,
and followed by a man from Christie's. She was carrying a small
cabinet, and the man had another and larger piece of furniture. She
almost ran in her ardour to carry her burden from one room to
another, and on her way she passed so near to the sewing friend
that she brushed her knee. Yet she did not appear to see her. The
friend took the cue, and ignored the presence of her hostess.
Normally it would have been good manners to offer to help in
carrying the various things which were being carried about; but it
was clear that as Mrs. Morrison had said she meant to be in bed
that morning—in bed she was. So she passed, again and again,
invisibly, while her friend invisibly sewed. At teatime she appeared as she had promised, and simply remarked that she had had
a restful morning, and that she hoped her guest had been happily
occupied.

In nothing did Mrs. Morrison show the true generosity of her
nature more than in the giving and receiving of presents. Most
noticeably in receiving, for the beautiful and gracious way in which
she showed pleasure in any little thing given to her by a friend was
indeed a more delicate movement of generosity than the making of
a gift herself. It was hard to think of things to give her, for she
seemed to have everything, and also she had the means to buy for
herself whatever she wanted; yet the difficulty that one felt was just
the measure of the difference between one's own generosity and
hers. She always appreciated the affection which prompted the
giving of a present to herself, but that was not all. She was really
delighted to open the parcel, for in spite of all her beautiful posses-
sions, to the end of her life she never became blasée. The thing

which she disentangled from its wrappings was at once in her eyes something fresh, surprising, interesting, ingenious, or beautiful.

The presents she gave were unique. A motor-car drove round Wiltshire a day or two before Christmas, leaving, not one parcel, but several, at the house of each of her friends. Accompanying them was a *catalogue raisonée* of the presents, for each thing had its own special feature, either in its appropriateness to the receiver, or in some historical or artistic interest of its own. These lists added immensely to the fun of unpacking the presents, for everything was described in most spirited style. The only occasion when I ever heard of any difficulty in reading Mrs. Morrison's most original and extremely clear handwriting, was when she seemed to describe a beautiful malacca walking-stick with a carved ivory top, as a 'Rabbiting Stick'. It couldn't have been that, but the stick remains a rabbiting stick to the present day.

Mrs. Morrison was completely indifferent as to the cost of the presents she gave, although she was well aware of the market value of things. No-one could judge better than she the probable price of a jewel, a piece of lace, a bit of furniture, an engraving, or a first edition. But when she gave a present, considerations of price did not concern her, one way or the other. She gave what she thought her friend wanted, and with no sparing of trouble to herself. With great care and the expenditure of considerable time, she would personally choose the model and arrange the fittings for a dress which would best bring out the points in a young girl whom she had invited to a party in her house, or for the wife of a composer whose opera was being produced in Brussels. She took infinite pains, when giving a fur coat to a poor lady who had never before possessed one, that it should not only be warm, but becoming. For an impecunious student living in the country, the present was a subscription to the London Library. But these presents were rich as well as appropriate, and it was the second of these characteristics which Mrs. Morrison really thought essential. At the door of a friend who had lately acquired a large empty house on the Berkshire downs there appeared one morning two pantechnicons filled with very valuable and beautiful eighteenth-century furniture. They came—like that— quite unexpectedly, without any parade or fuss. It meant that the new house, and any other house to be lived in by that friend in the future, must be for ever beautified by these rare things. And then the next morning came another present—this time a parcel by post. It was eagerly unpacked, and there appeared several pairs of what looked like vest sleeves without the vests. They had been considerably darned and mended, but were still able to keep the arms warm. Mrs. Morrison had been thinking again of that house on the downs, with the winds blowing round it. On winter nights she herself often wore, under her lace sleeves, a pair of these long woven mittens; and without waiting an hour she had gone to her room, and from her drawer had taken all she could find to send off in that parcel. In her eyes this present was every bit as important as the priceless furniture of the day before.

Mrs. Morrison did not exact or expect from the young the ideas or the standards of her own youth. What she appreciated in them was just that difference from her own youthful memories which to many old people is so annoying. She enjoyed drawing out her grandchildren and her other young friends, to learn from them what were, in their own eyes, the opinions and aims, the achievements and the failures of the new generation. 'Grand-Maye' they called her, as her own children had called her 'Maye'—the name given to her by her little girl Katharine, which lived on, as children's early attempts at speech so often do. So Mrs. Morrison remained to the end 'Maye' to more than one generation. It was characteristic of her that she could and did carry friendship over from one generation to another, and that, as the old friends died, their children and grandchildren grew up to claim what had fallen from their elders' hands. And it was easy to succeed to this inherited friendship, for Mrs. Morrison was that rare linguist—the one who understands and speaks a new version of her own native tongue.

The long and varied life, bringing the inevitable succession of losses of so many she had loved, did not wear down Mrs. Morrison's unfailing resiliency. She was indeed one of those who give fresh life to the hackneyed phrase, 'Age did not wither her nor custom stale her infinite variety'. And too, if she was ever tired, she would not lay that burden upon her friends. She adhered to her practice of only seeing them when she was at her best: otherwise she remained hidden in her own rooms. So to the last she met her visitors with the virile manner and quick grasp of things which had always distinguished her. Yet she must sometimes have longed for the end. In her youth she had been very impatient and she knew it; and during the last years she sometimes said to her daughter, 'I must wait and wait here till I have learnt the lesson of patience. Then I shall go.'

But she betrayed none of the weary quiescence which might sound in those words. She still dominated her dinner-table by her racy and sparkling conversation. She still talked with the same large gestures and free movements, ignoring such trifles as wine glasses and tumblers if they stood in her way. She would send half a dozen glasses crashing to the ground with a magnificent sweep of the hand, and appear absolutely unconscious of what she had done. The flow of her conversation continued unaffected by the din of breaking glasses; while Elliot, the perfect butler (whose dignity and distinction made Mrs. Morrison declare him to be a member of the St. Germains family) removed the wreckage, collecting the glasses in fragments from the floor, as naturally as he would have carried them whole from the table.

In religion, as in all else, Mrs. Morrison's attitude was individual. Throughout her life it occupied her deepest thoughts, but she was never dependent upon the rites of any church. She remained a member of the Church of England, in which her father had been a priest, and though she studied the teaching of the Church of Rome at the time when Lady Herbert of Lea and her daughter Lady Mary followed Newman and Manning into that communion, yet she could never have been at home there. Her whole personality had a colouring which gave her a strong outward affinity with the Latin races, yet her mind and intellect worked on lines which were distinctly English. Post-Reformation English too. Mrs. Morrison sometimes looked back to the undivided Western Church of the Middle Ages, and said that in a previous existence she had been a Catholic. But since the Reformation, both the Roman Church and the English mind have grown, and they have grown further apart. The elasticity of the Catholic Church has hardened at Rome into new dogmas; and the English people now think instinctively in terms of science. The ceremonies of the Church of Rome might have caught Mrs. Morrison's imagination: its tenets would have imprisoned her mind.

Mrs. Alfred Morrison

The thought of God possessed her, and she had the constant sense of His presence. Perhaps she found Him most nearly in human relationships; for she sometimes said that she disliked Thomas à Kempis because he taught that the disciple of Christ must be free from all bonds of personal affection. For her, human love was in each generation the incarnation afresh of Christ upon earth; and she certainly did give to such love always a touch of eternity.

When she was more than eighty years old, Mrs. Morrison decided to write a book. To begin at that age was characteristic of her, and of her courageous attitude in face of old age. Characteristic too was the idea of her book, indicating no loosening grip upon life, no world-weariness. Joy was her subject.

The book was to contain her ultimate philosophy of life—the sum of all she had learnt from experience, from reading, from thought and from prayer: and during the last years of her life it occupied her almost entirely. But she began too late. Time was against her. The strong masculine brain worked less easily. It became a battle with time, and in that battle she was beaten. The book was never finished, and the final and compelling occupation of those months bequeathed only a great sheaf of fragments. They have, in a way, a peculiar interest just because they *are* unfinished, for they show more of the working of the writer's mind.

What remained were two desks crammed with scraps of paper, postcards, exercise books, and notebooks, all completely covered with Mrs. Morrison's remarkable and unfailingly clear hand-writing. Almost all were written in pencil, and there is much less material in them than at first appears. Every passage, every phrase, and almost every word, has been weighed, considered, rewritten, altered, and corrected, with the most fastidious patience. And even in their final form, these unconnected passages did not represent the Mrs. Morrison who was known to her friends. They do not sound like her authentic and very individual utterances. In talk she had an audacity of phrase which gave to her conversation a very modern ring; while here are Victorian cadences, recalling the sixties and seventies, when Mrs. Morrison's literary taste was being formed. This is probably why she was never satisfied with what she wrote. It explains the constant and unfinished revision. She could not succeed in forcing the new wine into the old bottles.

Mrs. Alfred Morrison

So it was not possible to make a finished book from these bundles of notes without putting them into a new form, and one which Mrs. Morrison would neither have recognized nor accepted. A few inadequate extracts from them were printed some years ago for her friends, for if she had finished this book she meant it to be only for them. She wished to pass on what seemed to her to be the most precious thing which her long life had taught her—that sorrow is personal, and passes; while joy is universal, and remains.

LITANY OF PRAISE

For magpies in black and white array,
For velvet lawns where sunbeams chase and play,
For apple blossom gay garbed in pink and white,
For chestnut stately blooms, spring visions of delight,
For sunflowers, summer's golden heralds,
For the music of children's laughter echoing from their play,
For the wee wren softly singing,
    My tiny form and modest garb despise not.
    Gentle ways win many friends.
For summer's sunsets in radiant skies,
For dog's expressive eyes pleading for love's return,
For robins pugnacious to the feathered tribe, while friendly to our race,
For doves, soft cooing a lullaby to fairy babes,
For rosebuds red ensheathed in emerald moss,
For buttercups gold-lacquered gleaming in sunny meadows,
For owls, soft balls of fluff we fain would stroke,
For deep-hued violets appealing in their charm,
For birds stirring our hearts with their liquid notes of joy,
For the feathered rush of birds in spring,
For rustling leaves in autumn recalling the murmur of waiting crowds,
For the flush of rose rising on a summer evening from sea to sky,
For May blossom powdered pink,
For the orange blossom's bridal wreath,
For the Banksia rose of fairy elves,
For sweet peas redolent of perfume,
For the cuckoo's note, first harbinger of spring,
For soft-eyed primrose in tender yellow,

Mrs. Alfred Morrison

For daisies irrepressible in desire to live,
For laburnum with its sunkissed tresses,
For white lilacs tasselled in lace,
For roses, queens of scent and colour,
For the cowslip balls we toss,
For the fragrance of golden gorse,
For the swallows acclaimed with joy,
For snowdrops smiling at winter's passing,
For radiant tulips of regal mien,
For water lilies rooted in tranquil stream,
For lilies of the valley, their white bells pealing,
For the music of children's laughter in their games at play,
For the pink-hosed chattering seagulls,
For forget-me-nots fringing with blue the summer meadows,
For harebells, unconscious of charm, swayed by the summer breeze,
For wheat fields in August sun, the late gold of the fading summer,
For Madonna lilies regal in beauty and sovereign purity,
For the mystic passion flower recalling Gothic art,
For the clematis wreathing garlands for the waning year,
For the sky starred with glory,
For the sun's gleaming mirror, the sparkling sea,
For the dewdrops changing with every morning, seeming sometimes like
*   jewels dropped by a vanished rainbow,*
For daisies sprinkled on the lawn,
For softly scented honeysuckles,
For peonies in royal red,
All these I praise in song.
*   The great chorus of praise Earth ever yields to Heaven.*

MISS
BARBARA TOWNSEND

Salisbury Spire has often been compared to a finger pointing heavenward out of the great undulating spaces of Salisbury Plain; and if this is a good analogy, never was a finger decorated with so unique a ring of gems. As is well known, the cathedral was built in thirty years: it was a sudden uprush of genius. But the Close grew round it very slowly during the following eight centuries, and in its seventy-four houses can be read the whole history of English domestic architecture.

In Salisbury, this history begins in the days of Bishop Poore, who founded the cathedral in 1220. The great crypt in the palace was his hall; and there still exist in the Close the two small houses in which lived Elias de Dereham, the clerk of the works, and Robert the mason, who together conceived and created the great building. And while the cathedral slowly grew out of the marshland around it, the two builders made themselves these unpretentious little houses. The contrast between what they thought fitting as a House of God and as a house for a man recalls a remark made by a little boy of three who, looking up at the cathedral for the first time, said, 'They must have had *a lot of stuff* to build that big church'. They had indeed.

Mary's meadow, upon which the cathedral was built, was the

property of Bishop Poore; and when he came down from Old Sarum with his Chapter, he gave special privileges to those canons who built and presented to the cathedral 'Houses of Residence' for themselves and their successors. This is why the Close houses for the first three centuries have each a character of its own. From the first, Salisbury Close welcomed individual taste in those who built within its walls. Later on, in the seventeenth and eighteenth centuries, the urbane and far-sighted canons of the day encouraged country gentlemen from the neighbourhood to make themselves houses in the Close. This is how it happened that in the time of Wren and his immediate successors, when English architecture was at its zenith, there were placed within the walls of Salisbury Close most of the houses which now give to it its placid and yet startling beauty. The most beautiful of these was Mompesson House, built in 1701.

This was the house in which Barbara Townsend was born almost exactly in the middle of the nineteenth century, and it was her home for the whole of her life, which lasted ninety-seven years.

The Close houses seem to have a remarkable effect on their owners. A community mainly consisting of clergymen and old ladies does not sound a promising forcing ground for unusual personalities, yet Salisbury Close has always abounded in these. G. M. Young, in his *Portrait of an Age*, speaks of 'the life of the university-bred classes of the mid-nineteenth century' as having been, 'the culminating achievement of European culture', and he finds its final stronghold 'in that walled close where all the pride and piety, the peace and beauty of a vanished world seem to have made their home under the spire of Saint Mary of Salisbury'.

When Barbara Townsend died in 1939, she had shown to a new generation and to a new century a very exquisite personality coming out of that 'culminating achievement'. This meant that the end of her life was rather solitary. Surrounded as she was with love and admiration, she lived a little apart from the people about her. The Close itself was her nearest intimate. It alone had come with her out of the remote past. The spire with the moon and the stars moving about it, and with the peregrines building their nests within it: the blue and purple crocuses which grew in the gardens in the spring: the canons' houses, each of which had outlived a succession of distinguished clerics since the ones she remembered as a little child: the famous row of limes opposite to the windows of Mompesson House, which were felled during her old age—these things were really her familiars, in spite of the ease with which she outwardly adapted herself to the various generations growing up round her. For her increasing deafness did not prevent her from so adapting herself, and her fresh and independent mind often seemed more modern than the youth who clustered about her. This was because she represented a generation which expected its members to be individual. 'The university-bred classes of the nineteenth century' were an independent lot, even if they lived in a walled-in close, the gates of which were (and still are) locked every night at eleven o'clock. Barbara Townsend coming from this generation, had a mind of her own; and naturally and courteously she spoke her mind to the last.

Barbara was the second of the four children of Mr. George Barnard Townsend, who, about the year 1840, acquired the lease of Mompesson House, which till then had been occupied by some member of the Portman family. He was a solicitor who played an influential part in transactions concerned with the acquisition of land for railways, the great new development of the day. He was a sportsman, a famous cricketer playing for Gentlemen *v.* Players in the days when amateurs played in tall hats. He was also an enthusiastic yachtsman, and had a little property near the sea at Mudeford, which was within driving distance of Salisbury. He married his next-door neighbour in the Close, a Miss Eyre, and when she died a few years later, a doorway was cut in the wall between two houses, thus making them one. The other Miss Eyre had still been living with her father next door, and now she could mother her nephew and her three little nieces.

This was the party which occupied Mompesson House for between twenty and thirty years. Jenny, the second of the girls, kept a journal after she left the schoolroom, and from this, one can get an impression of the daily life of the young ladies who lived in the Close at that time. When the Townsends were in Salisbury we read how they walked in the Close and 'met the Husseys and had a good laugh'; or else they 'had a very jolly walk on the terrace on Harnham hill'. Often they leaned out of the window at night, revelling in the beauty of the spire bathed in the quiet moonlight. A more festive occasion was an archery party at the Pinckneys', when Jenny's score was thirteen out of forty-five. Not too good, one would think, but it did not prevent the whole thing from being 'very jolly'. There was a great deal of dancing in the neighbourhood, at country houses like Clarendon or Ferne and sometimes in the Salisbury Assembly Rooms or at the White Hart Hotel. Jenny enjoyed this last dance very much, but her sisters were more critical, pronouncing the room too long and narrow and the floor sticky. The music and the sermons in the cathedral made a great part of the lives of everyone in the Close. They were discussed, praised, disapproved, analysed, criticized, and written about. Jenny often wrote from memory long extracts from the sermon she had heard on a Sunday afternoon, and she applied these to her own life in a completely sincere and naïve manner. These 'jolly' and laughing girls all seemed to be very conscious that the cathedral and the faith for which it stood were something far greater than themselves. The aim of the pointing finger was higher than the ring which surrounded it.

The Townsends drove about the roads of the neighbourhood in the family landau. Very often, however, their drives went beyond the regular circuit of the Downton or Laverstock roads and, stepping into 'the spider', they bowled away for thirty miles to Mudeford, there to stay for a few weeks. The journal has tender descriptions of the moonlit beauty of the sea coast near Christchurch and of the stars in the deep blue sky. One morning in November, Jenny writes, 'It was delightful to sit out before breakfast and to see such a lovely scene'; for the beauty of nature was always the chief pleasure of life for these girls.

There were days when Mr. Townsend went away leaving the girls to amuse themselves alone, and then they took the punt or a light rowing boat that could easily be managed, and went across to the Haven where the fishermen lived. Here they had started a little school for the children, and the two younger sisters used to teach in it all the morning, after which they visited and made friends with the mothers. Barbara usually spent the whole of these days sketching near the sea.

There were cruises with 'Pappy' in his tiny yacht, the *Gundimore*, which sometimes ended with unexpected though pleasurable excitement, for Jenny mentions quite by the way 'the wind and the tide blew us aground' and they could not get home till they were rescued by 'a party from the steamer'. When 'Pappy' went away, Francis, a smart and entertaining young cousin, took them out 'in the four-oar' for 'all sorts of adventures'; and Mudeford was often the scene of great parties of cousins of all degrees when the fun grew fast and furious.

The Townsends generally had a house in Belgravia for three months in the spring, and they enjoyed their London season in a quiet way. It always began by 'driving and leaving a lot of cards'; and on Sundays they walked in the Park, of course, and sat there between the services at Saint Andrew's or Saint Peter's. They went to small parties like the one given by the George Spotteswoods, when 'Mrs. S. and Mrs. A. sang some very pretty duets'. Music was always a great joy, and one afternoon they found a great crowd in Saint James's Hall when Arabella Goddard, who gave lessons to Barbara at Salisbury, played the piano, and when Patti sang 'most beautifully'. They heard a Haydn quartet played by Joachim's party at a Monday Pop, and on that day Sims Reeves sang 'most exquisitely'. They were not, however, content with only hearing music, and while they were in London they took the opportunity of themselves having singing lessons. Jenny writes proudly that 'the master thinks our voices improved'.

A party given by the Horticultural Society was also most enjoyable. It took place in a gigantic conservatory decorated with 'splendid shrubs' and there was 'a brilliant band of gas lights round the top of the wall'. Everyone was in full dress and a band played in the passage. The Duke of Buccleugh received the guests who were all presented to him. The Townsends 'met a few friends' and got home about midnight.

Every year they went often to the Academy where the great names were Millais, Leighton, Landseer, and Sant; and they loved going to Christie's sales. But on the whole a London season sounds less amusing than a Salisbury one.

When George, the handsome soldier brother, married Miss Frances Bulteel, his sisters went of course to Plymouth for the wedding. They stayed at the Royal Hotel, though they had most meals with the Bulteels who gave them very good dinners, followed by 'pleasant evenings' when the family sang 'very well'. There was a 'fine set-out of presents' and the wedding was followed by an enormous wedding breakfast. In the evening they had a family high tea when games of consequences were 'good fun'. George was a wonderful figure at the service in the smartest of all the uniforms of the day, the brilliant full dress of the Horse Artillery. The bridesmaids wore double skirts of white tulle over white silk, trimmed with a double row of roses. On their heads were rose-coloured velvet coronets from which hung white veils. In their hands they carried the presents given them by the bridegroom which were scent bottles of rose-coloured glass with gold tops. Frances 'looked lovely in an exquisite dress of white satin and Honiton lace and there was hardly any crying so all went off capitally though poor little Francie cried a great deal when they went away of course'. This was in spite of her charming costume of dove-coloured silk with a black and white jacket trimmed with black cord and her bonnet of ivy and horse daisies with 'a tatted veil made by cousin Cooey'.

When the three sisters got back to the hotel that night, they were still in such high spirits that they had 'fun' in their bedroom and 'got into bed very late'.

Clothes often appear in the journal and were nearly always of the same delicate colours. Of course when the Duchess of Kent died they all wore black and white checks, black hats and gloves, and black bands. When Barbara was left free to choose for herself, she wore a light dove silk frock with little pinked flowers coming halfway up the skirt, and over this a white shawl trimmed with black lace. On the days before parties the girls spent a good deal of time making wreaths of natural flowers to be worn in the hair; and not only for themselves, as the journal says that one day they 'came in and made wreaths for Aunt Jane to go to the party in'. How pretty those wreaths must have been.

The Townsends occasionally went abroad but they never seem to have gone farther afield than Florence and the Italian and French Rivieras.

In her hundreds and thousands of water-colour drawings and oil paintings, her painted china, and her tiles, Barbara Townsend left behind her a record of her life for all to see. These paintings do not only represent things which struck her on one day or another, as subjects for pictures. They were her whole life. It was that pictorial outlook on the world—clear, distinct, yet visionary—which gave to her eyes when you met her in the Close a look as though she could always see something very vividly, but something that was just out of the reach of everyone else.

Her visits to the Continent must of course have meant a good deal to her, and all her life she kept in touch with the art world of London, but her real genius lay in things far more original and personal. Her great aesthetic achievement was so to fill with her imagination three or four subjects, that they sufficed to bring before future generations the whole of the ninety-six years of her life. These subjects of hers were Salisbury Cathedral and Close, the sea and the river at Mudeford, the moon and the stars over the spire or above the cool curves of the downs, and a few flowers. It is true that there are some animated groups of tiny figures on beaches in the south of France, and a brilliant series of drawings made at some artillery manœuvres in Ireland. These were subjects which naturally appealed to her gift of draughtsmanship, but what made her an artist was her unique power of going back and back to the same place, always to find something fresh—to Mudeford, to the Odstock Downs, to the Close, to the crescent moon, or to the azaleas flowering every year in great pots in the hall at Mompesson. It was, perhaps, characteristic of many Victorians to absorb into their bones the details of what now appear rather monotonous lives, and to find those lives worth living; but Barbara Townsend's pictures show this characteristic raised to the point of genius.

In her youth the Close had quite a large population of girls and they were most of them girls of taste. Bishop Hamilton had a family of eight, and his successor, Bishop Moberly, had fifteen children. There were Husseys, Heathcotes, Gordons, Jacobs, and, as visitors, countless Awdry relations of the Moberlys. Everybody had cousins to stay for weeks at a time. It was the fashion of the day. Most of the girls drew and painted; and Barbara's only drawing lessons were given to her at this time, by Mrs. James Hussey, who organized sketching parties for these enthusiastic young lovers of art. Some of Barbara's early pictures were portraits of the Close dwellers of those days, groups of girls wearing crinolines or full-gathered skirts in some of the much loved delicate shades of dove-colour and grey. Barbara used to say that the clothes of that date were lessons in deportment; as it required two hands, two feet, and all the body skilfully aligned before it was possible, in a crinoline, to pass modestly through the little white wooden posts placed close together at the entrance to the Cathedral green. It was easier for a camel to go through the eye of a needle than for an unpractised crinoline wearer to squeeze gracefully through those unyielding little poles. The unwary woman who tried to compress her skirt sufficiently to make it the right width found that the unnaturally narrowed hoop sprang up over her head, leaving her legs blushingly displayed in modest white cambric drawers with lace frills.

Those early days in the Close were wonderfully carefree, and the Townsend sisters had a gay and happy life; but a lifetime of ninety-seven years must possess as its landmarks a great many tomb-stones. These began to mark Barbara Townsend's road from a very early stage. Her mother had died so soon that she can never have been anything but a grave to her children, but both Mr. Townsend and his sister-in-law also died when the daughters were still young women. Some surprise was then felt when the sisters went off to Switzerland with no chaperone but their old nurse, and when they returned they sought no other duenna. But the elderly spinsters who were their neighbours soon agreed that the Close itself was chaperone enough; though even if this had not been the case, the Townsends would have gone their own way. The death of George, the only brother, was an agonizing grief. This beautiful artillery officer lives in many of Barbara's brilliant little drawings; and in Jenny's description in the diary of his driving away after the wedding 'in a carriage with post horses' while 'poor little Francie' sat at his side 'in floods of tears'. George's looks were of the romantic dazzling kind which tells of consumption and he died of a sudden haemorrhage at only thirty-two years of age.

Remember that these were the days of Victoria, the widowed Queen, when there was a general trend towards graveyards, and so it is not surprising that, after these deaths, the life of the Townsend sisters was for many years focused upon the cathedral cloister. This is perhaps the most beautiful churchyard in England. The cloisters lie on the south side of the cathedral; and like the spire, they date from a century later than the main building with its unspoilt early English lines. The cloisters are less severe than the building itself, being in the playful Decorative style. Two great cedars break the level turf of the little square enclosure, and the four hundred feet of the spire leap up almost directly above it. There is no place from which it has a more impressive effect. The graves are level with the ground and marked by very small flat stones; so the frequent journeys to the graves of Father, Mother, Aunt, and Brother were, for these girls who loved every stone of the cathedral, far less morbid than they sound. And all this time, Barbara continued to draw and paint.

Now followed the family romance. Jenny fell in love with Willie Hammick, a distant cousin, who, after the manner of lovers in those days, was too much of a gentleman to declare himself without the previous approval of the father of the family. George, of course, had taken that position from the point of view of a would-be suitor, and when he died, Mr. Hammick was left in doubt as to what was the right thing to do. He decided to go off to America on a business journey without having spoken, and while there he had a very serious illness which kept him in bed in New York for many months. Jenny's diary, at this crisis, relapses into German characters, for she could not resist writing down her feelings, and yet a complete reserve about love affairs was *de rigueur* among the refined young ladies of the day. The writing is therefore often illegible, but even so these volumes make a poem. Reticence or not, Jenny was impelled to let her heart speak, and the heart that speaks is as pure and clear as crystal. She frankly admits that she adores this man, who so far had only treated her as a cousin. Jenny's sisters knew what was going on, but they too possessed the well-bred reticence, so her only outlet was her diary, and Barabara continued to sketch. Her drawings grew better and better.

When Willie at last came home, he realized that no gentleman could possibly propose to a young girl when it was probable that he was doomed to be a cripple for life. For such was the prospect before him. He would now be unable to follow his profession, and Jenny was something of an heiress. Another well-mannered interval of silence was indicated, and this wordless love affair had lasted for four years in all before the lovers were married. There was no white satin wedding dress and no crowd of bridesmaids in tulle dresses, no gay wedding breakfast. The ceremony took place at eight o'clock in the morning in Christ Church, Lancaster Gate. It had indeed been a tragic waste of time, for in less than four more years Jenny was dead after the birth of her son, and she left three tiny children to grow up in Mompesson House. History had repeated itself. Once more there was a motherless family to be brought up by their aunts.

In course of time, Mr. Hammick became a leading figure in Salisbury. He was Mayor and Alderman, as well as the most prominent member of the Conservative Party, and he was soon made organizer to the party in the county division outside. Mompesson was filled with ardent local politicians. During elections, much of the work was carried on in the house and many envelopes addressed. Barbara sometimes joined in this routine work, but this was only from kindness of heart. Her general attitude, though sympathetic, was aloof. She was friendly to these strangers with their loud voices who so unexpectedly haunted her home; but she was not much interested in the views so loudly expressed by those voices. In fact, in that centre of toryism she remained something of a heretic. It was not only in the fashion of her gowns, in her taste in furniture, and in her style of painting that she was serenely independent of everyone about her. She was equally so in her views on religion and public affairs and in the conduct of her private life. She thought as she liked; and when she spoke, she spoke as she thought. But she was entirely free from the rude mindlessness of the commonplace person who says 'I always speak my mind' and then has no mind to speak. In days when conversation on 'difficult' subjects was taboo in drawing-rooms, Barbara Townsend openly and strongly approved of what she called the 'common sense' of cremation; she was violently opposed to submarines; she looked on divorce as a completely possible means of exit from an impossible marriage; and she enunciated her socialistic views in the very presence of her brother-in-law.

But though she spoke freely and well upon all of these subjects they never seemed to her to be the things that mattered most in life. She could always return to her painting.

Miss Barbara Townsend

One by one, the companions of her youth were dying, and Barbara lived on. Jenny's two little girls grew up, so another generation of the 'young ladies of the Close' ran in and out of Mompesson House, chattering about their tennis, their dancing, and their love affairs. The two girls married, and in a tragically short time each of them returned as a widow bringing an only child to be brought up by the aunts at Mompesson. Last of all, Gertrude, Barbara's younger sister died too; and now there were three generations, each consisting of one member, to share the great house where they had all had such fun in their time.

During the last twenty years of her life, Barbara Townsend unconsciously became an almost legendary figure in the Close. Strangers often asked the name of the lady who wandered, always alone, into the cathedral at any hour during any service. The place appeared to belong to her, in the same definite yet impersonal way in which it belonged to the head verger or to the dean. She seemed apart from the passing day. Her appearance had its own beauty. A small trim figure with a resolute gait, she walked about, swathed in cloaks, capes, shawls, scarves, and veils, superimposed one over the other, and falling behind her in graceful disarray. Her features were small and finely cut, her mouth firm, her eyes intent. She had a quiet voice, and spoke distinctly.

And should the inquiring stranger summon up courage to follow this fascinating figure back to Mompesson House, asking permission to look behind its exquisite façade, he would be neither snubbed nor disappointed. Barbara was quite spontaneously on easy terms with any person, stranger or otherwise who, like herself, was in quest of beauty. The Close ladies all took it for granted that visitors desired to see the inside of their houses, and Mompesson had been a 'show place' even before that cliché was coined.

Barbara Townsend's immense appreciation of the beauty of her house was quite other than that present-day affectation which consists in treating such a place as a 'period piece', and disposing in it a few choice bits of furniture correct to the very decade. Not at all. Miss Townsend used her home to live in and she filled the hall with her works of art, finished or unfinished, with her great pots of azaleas, her little pots of crocuses, her paint box and camp stool, her hat, veil, and goloshes. And yet the whole effect was surprisingly harmonious. And the little sitting-room was similar. It was crowded with the harvest of Barbara's long life. Till her last weeks she was still busy, making things, tending her plants, baking her pottery, and, sitting indoors or in the outside court, painting, and painting, and painting. She painted the subjects which from her girlhood she had made her own—the moon floating round the spire as it had floated in the bygone days of Mrs. Hussey's sketching classes; the stars for ever entangled in the branches of the trees; the little flowers which were always ready to group themselves in vague patterns on her tiles. She loved the pale blues and the roseate hues of the sky at dawn and gradually the whole house was pervaded by these delicate tones. Sofas, tables, and chairs were stacked with half-finished drawings and paintings in faint shades of pale blue, green, and pink. Tiles lay in heaps on the floor in every corner. Teacups in process of painting seemed to have been forgotten on all the window seats. When the end came, at nearly ninety-seven years of age, one felt that Barbara Townsend had been too soon snatched away in the middle of her countless occupations. Her achievement was colossal, even reckoning with the many years of that long life. But her greatest achievement was to have shown to a world muddled in the twentieth-century problems of war and peace, of organization and planning, the kind of life which was lived by a Victorian lady in Salisbury Close more than eighty years before.

MRS. PERCY WYNDHAM

'All gone. Alas! Alas!'

These words were written by Madeline Wyndham on a tiny amateur photograph of Burne-Jones's great mural painting of a multitude of angels which covered the staircase wall in the first Clouds House. This was built by her husband at East Knoyle in Wiltshire during the ten years ending in 1885. The hall and staircase came to their end in a fire which practically destroyed the house within three years of its building, so the little epitaph might have applied from the first to more than the painting itself.

Those prosperous Victorian days saw rising, in many parts of the country, the last great batch of English country houses. People were rich in those days, and families were large, so building was in fashion. Clouds was considered the masterpiece of Philip Webb, one of the leading architects of the day. It had a short, brilliant, catastrophic existence, fit for the descendants of Edward Fitzgerald, for Madeline Wyndham was a grandchild of that fascinating and fated figure. After the burning of the house, the Wyndhams at once rebuilt it on exactly the same plan. The original workmen were recalled, and each man was given again the same piece of work that he had finished in the original house. While this went on, the family camped in the enormous 'servants' wing', which they found

F*

extremely comfortable for, as they remarked, the architect was fortunately a socialist. For fifty years or more the rebuilt Clouds stood on its highland, an emblem of some of the outstanding aspects of Victorian aristocracy: its opulent assured presentation of a dignified home life; its patronage of the arts; its large hospitality; and its natural assumption of the leadership of rural life. The Wyndhams designed it thinking that it was destined to shelter many successive generations of their family; for if there was any one thing of which the Victorians were more calmly certain than of anything else, it was of the permanence of their own way of life. Progress they accepted as a universal law—a 'progress slowly broadening down from precedent to precedent'. That had been assured to them by Professor Darwin, and by the latest school of historians who built their philosophy upon his doctrine of evolution. Lord Tennyson had raised these theories of science and of history to the level of poetic vision. People of all schools of thought were now convinced that the world had for ever moved away from the Age of Barbarism. If a war was heard of, it always took place a very long way off, in some remote continent which had not yet come under the beneficent sway of Queen Victoria's pacific sceptre.

And now? "All gone. Alas! Alas!"

Madeline Wyndham was of romantic descent. Her grandmother was the celebrated Pamela, thought to be the daughter of Madame de Genlis and Philip Egalité. Pamela married Lord Edward Fitzgerald, who died as a revolutionary in a Dublin prison in 1798. They had two daughters, one of whom—another Pamela—married Sir Guy Campbell, an attractive and impecunious Scottish baronet, with whom she lived happily, but not 'ever afterwards', for Sir Guy died in less than twenty years, leaving his widow with eleven children and an income of £600 a year. Lady Campbell was a delightful, happy-go-lucky, unpractical creature, whose life was summed up by her friend Miss Emily Eden as being 'full of Irish and English fun and misery, adventures and difficulties'.

This was the household from which Mrs. Wyndham came. Madeline was the seventh and youngest of Lady Campbell's daughters, and in 1860 she married Percy, the younger son of the first Lord Leconfield. When the parents were making business arrangements before the wedding (a serious matter in those days when trustees and marriage settlements were even more important matrimonial preliminaries than choosing the parson and the wedding ring) Lady Campbell wrote to the bridegroom's father: 'On my death, the girls will each have fifty pounds a year, and that is all, so you must be content with Madeline's good qualities as her portion.'

They were indeed a sufficient dowry. Madeline Campbell was a captivating jumble of genius, beauty, and charm, derived from her mixed French, Irish, Scottish, and English ancestry. As life went on, her vital spirit compounded this legacy of varied qualities into a personality rich in intelligence, sympathy, and wit. She had in fact every characteristic which could make the perfect hostess.

The Wyndhams had been married for some years before they found what they had looked for from the first. This was a site for the house they meant to build, and the one they chose was indeed a magnificent one. It stood among those wide uplands which form the south-west corner of Wiltshire. The sole remaining tower of Beckford's Fonthill stands on a neighbouring summit; a few miles to the north-west, King Alfred's Tower above Stourhead dominates many miles of the Wiltshire and Somerset landscape; while to the south stands Shaftesbury on the last jutting spur of the Dorset hills.

The building of the house took ten years, and during this time the Wyndhams made their home at Wilbury, an eighteenth-century house about thirty miles away, where the last of their five children were born, so that when Clouds was ready, they took possession of it as a complete household of the period. At last they had reached the end of those constant drives backwards and forwards over the downs to watch the progress of the building, and now they were established for life. Although they visited Knoyle on a great many occasions during those ten years, there was one particular day when no member of the family was present. Legend says that while the final touches were being given to the house a mysterious old woman, clothed in shabby black, appeared to one of the workmen. Holding up her hand like some ancient sorceress she said these words:

'In three years' time this house will not be standing.'

She vanished, and was never seen again; so when the Wyndhams took possession a few months later, they knew nothing of the curse which had been pronounced on their new home.

Mrs. Percy Wyndham

The cold of the winter of 1888 was a legend throughout the south of England for over a generation. On January the 6th of that year, very early in the morning, a sleepy servant put into a housemaid's cupboard a scuttleful of the ashes which she had just scraped out of the fireplace of the night before. Unfortunately they were not all dead, and there was paper in the scuttle too. By seven o'clock the whole house was ablaze, the fire roaring up through the great central hall, which went sheer from the ground floor to the roof. It made a perfect funnel through which a strong current of air drove the flames with incredible force. When it was discovered, little could be done. There were then no telephones. The telegraph service did not operate at night. Salisbury was twenty miles away, and Mere, the nearest place, was separated from Clouds by roads which were practically impassable through the frost. Grooms on galloping horses went out from the stables and scoured the country for the fire engines, which in that remote country district were then manhandled, and only adapted for very small village fires. So while the fire roared on uninterrupted, it took hours to reach the nearest horse-drawn engines, one of which was stationed at Salisbury and another at Wilton, where Lord Pembroke had an estate fire brigade. The Pembrokes were close friends of the Wyndhams. No-one could be more willing to send help, but the difficulties were beyond anything we can imagine to-day. Clouds stands above Wilton by more than the height of Salisbury spire, and the hills between the two places are very steep. The roads that morning were like glass, and three times in the course of that eighteen-mile journey the horses fell on a specially steep gradient, and were too badly hurt to go on. They were replaced by fresh teams, borrowed from near-by farms. Thus reinforced they sped along again, slipping and sliding about the roads, and seeing ahead of them, all the time, the enormous pillar of fire which Clouds had now become. When they arrived it was almost a hopeless case, for the fire had got full possession and the flames appeared almost to reach the sky. It was still freezing so hard that the captain of the Wilton brigade—a gigantic man of great strength—was almost frozen to death as he stood on the roof directing the hose. To anyone watching from the ground, his figure was clearly silhouetted against the fire in the background. And after a time it appeared to lose its mobility and erect carriage.

MRS. MORRISON, AGED EIGHTY-FIVE
from a photograph by Debenham & Gould Ltd.

MRS. PERCY WYNDHAM
from the painting by Sir William Orpen in the possession of Lord
Leconfield

Mrs. Percy Wyndham

What had happened to Captain Carse? A fireman approached him, and took his arm. It was completely stiff. And then it transpired that his clothes, which were saturated with water, had turned to ice even in the midst of the fire and Carse was frozen on to the side of the ladder up which he had climbed.

Meanwhile the household, the estate men, and the village people all played their parts. The family escaped by the skin of their teeth. Some small grandchildren were in the nursery at the very top of the house, and they were swathed in wet blankets with sponges in their mouths, and carried downstairs by their nurses, whose shoes were all but burnt through on the red-hot stairs.

The village people rushed in and out of the burning building, dragging out everything that they thought of value. The priceless furniture and *objets d'art* were heaped helter-skelter in the garden. The rustics considered the billiard table to be the rarest thing in the house, and this was tenderly salvaged and lugged out on to the lawn. At all the bedroom windows there appeared the determined faces of distracted housemaids hurling the jugs and basins and bedroom crockery down from the top floors on to the ground, till Mrs. Wyndham interrupted this well-meant though disastrous clatter, by saying that she thought it was not worth while to 'save any more china'.

As the pale winter sun came up over the garden, she was seen standing a little way off from the ruins of the house, with a rapt look on her face, as she watched the glorious curved tongues of flame which leapt from the burning walls into the sky. She had thrown a rough homespun coat over her nightgown, and the lace frills escaped beneath the tweed sleeves and fell over her hands which were flung out in an unconscious gesture of wonder at the sight. She was entranced by its beauty and terror.

The new house was at once begun and, like its predecessor, it was built of green sandstone. This is the soil of the district, which now blossomed into a mellow building material as naturally as it made a perfect foundation for a garden. The great hall, through which the fire had swept so mercilessly on that icy morning, once again soared from the ground floor to the red tiled roof; but in future it would echo the strains of music instead of the blast of flames. This hall contained an organ loft, but it never had an organ in it, although almost every other instrument was heard there. The walls were lined with unstained oak, and the house contained the interesting collection of eighteenth-century furniture which the Wyndhams had amused themselves by making since their marriage. But they were never content to live only among period pieces. They were friends and patrons of the most famous artists and craftsmen of their own day. Not only were the works of contemporary artists to be seen at Clouds and in Belgrave Square but the artists themselves made Madeline's parties remarkable. The Burne-Jones family were great friends, as were the Leightons, Watts, Val Princeps, William Morris, Sargent, and many more. Madeline took lessons from Alexander Fisher in enamelling, and she became skilled at this work, successfully combining miniature painting with her enamels. She loved the surprises which are created by the enamellist's oven when the original colours are almost completely changed as the fire takes the bit between its teeth. She was never tired of making things in this effective medium, and all about her she encouraged Victorian craftsmen. The Royal School of Art Needlework was founded by her and her neighbour Mrs. Alfred Morrison, under the patronage of Princess Christian.

There was this great difference between the rich people of the immediate pre-war period and their predecessors, the rich Victorian ladies. The Victorians were active amateurs. They loved and practised the arts, as people of taste can seldom do in these days, when they come up everywhere against the amateur turned professional, who always seems to do everything better than they. In spite of the many great artists who came in and out of her house in London or in the country, Mrs. Wyndham and her contemporaries fearlessly decorated their houses themselves. When they went on their travels abroad or to out-of-the-way parts of the British Isles, they collected treasures of all sorts—woven silks, hand-spun woollens, Italian printed paper, hand-made lace; and in their houses were cabinets, cupboards, and chests of drawers packed with the spoils of the chase. When they meant to cover a chair or a sofa, they rummaged among these stores, pulling out their beautiful brocades, piling them in heaps on the floor and going down on their knees to worship the colours and designs, and to choose what they wanted. Then they cut out the covers for their sofas and chairs, stitching them with the help of their maids. The only 'professional' who was sometimes called in was a visiting upholstress in the neighbourhood, who would stay in the house for weeks at a time, to work under the direct supervision of the lady of the house. The effect was a less planned whole than is achieved by the famous decorators of the past thirty years, for such people did not then exist. But it had its charm, and Victorian rooms were often a riot of unexpected colour arranged by someone with an unerring eye.

Here are some extracts from a letter written by Mrs. Wyndham to her daughter Madeline Adeane, which show the fervent yet casual way in which the Victorians tackled the decoration of their rooms:

'I send you a bit of cheap cream damask to make a table cover for the table that you put the yellow silk on *wrong side out*. I think there might be enough of it to cut off for the long seat, but am not quite sure. I am making (or having made!) a green common silk cover for your big table and it shall be sent by post to-morrow I *hope*, but if it does not come in time, you must make a big cover of this cream damask for it, and leave the yellow silk wrong side out on the little round table. It really does not look bad. I send you a bit of red which you can use anywhere in your sitting or bedroom—a *remnant* and also two turkish embroidered squares for *anywhere*—tablecloths, or just to put over any of the red chairs, that stand near and swear with *the greens*! I send a bit of green silk, seven yards, and some thin flannel to line it with, to cover the *long seat* if you cannot use the cream damask. You will have to join the flannel. It is all I had. *It is safest* to make up one *big* tablecloth with the cream damask, big enough for the big table [a drawing here] one width in middle half width on each side in case the green one *does not come in time*, then you can use it on any table afterwards. Perhaps the green will not suit or match with the lovely Italian green piano cover. I fear *it will not*, and if so, *the cream will look best in the room*. Put the green *on some bed*, if it does not match in the drawing-room.'

That is all very typical of Mrs. Wyndham's breathless interest in every little mat on every little table in the houses of her beloved daughters. It is extremely funny to read to-day, and to imagine those rooms crowded with hangings made from wonderful pieces of brocade joined together in widths and half-widths, and lined with 'thin flannel'.

The flowers in the rooms at Clouds or at Belgrave Square testified to the skill of the Wyndhams' gardeners, but not to their taste, which was always that of Mrs. Wyndham herself. Those groups of orange-trees, hydrangeas, camellias, and lilacs in the corners of the rooms were Madeline Wyndham's choice and no-one else's. Near these clumps of flowering shrubs always hung the wicker cage housing the doves which went with her everywhere. In those days there was a fashion in 'dinner-table arrangement' which has won permanently the hearts of the exhibitors and judges of every village flower show. This consisted of slender glass vases dotted all over the table and connected by ropes of smilax. Madeline's taste was different. She placed nothing but a single bowl of flowers in the middle of her table.

Among the treasures which Victorian ladies used to bring home from Italy were reams upon reams of printed Florentine paper in rich colourings. Madeline Wyndham was an enthusiast for these, and in them she bound many of her commonplace books. She also used vellum for her book covers, beautifying it with her own paintings and illuminations. These commonplace books made for her a kind of diary of the mind, and she always had one or more of them in the process of being filled with drawings, poems, and quotations. Here can be found the deepest things that she carried in her heart, and the clue to the secret of her happiness. No-one could be long with Mrs. Wyndham without being struck by her ardent love and zest for life; yet these books reveal that the thought of death too was never far away. She had no fear of it. On the contrary, the memory of death gave to the passing hours their supreme value for her.

On a page of one of her books she writes: 'The "departed" only *go* from this world. Like the dolorous knight they hear the voice of death as that of a messenger who brought pleasant news, or like Saint Francis of Assisi they "go to meet death singing". For the dead we grieve not, but our Tablet for them is the Tablet in the Catacombs which records the death of Eutychia as "Happiest of Women". With Plato we can say of our dead, "I did not weep for him, but for my own future as being deprived of such a friend", or with Michael Angelo after the death of Urbino: "you know how Urbino died. It is a mark of God's great goodness, yet a bitter grief to me." It was not the natural, human or right sorrow at the loss and deprivation that Saint Cyprian girded at, it was the selfish brooding, self-enclosed grief, so hurtful to self, so hindering to others, that he was reproving.' Among all these quotations she leads up to this climax:

'Be comforted, dear madam.'

'No I will not. All strange and terrible things are welcome, but comforts we despise.'

On the first page of one of these manuscript books is a wonderful lyrical passage in which she sees life at its summit only when it is crowned by death. The page was very carefully written in a beautiful script, and evidently meant much to her as a young woman. Years afterwards, when the happy life at Clouds was over, and she was a widow in her London house, the last blow fell on her—the death of her son George. Then she dedicated one of her books to his memory and she cut this page from the early volume, putting it in the forefront of the new book, and writing beneath it, in her generous shapely hand, this extract:

'Dead. But triumphant. I progress on.'

Truly, as she wrote in her Bible, 'Vision is the art of seeing things invisible'.

This was Madeline Wyndham's inner life, while outwardly she seemed to be simply making a worldly success during that quarter of a century of which it has been written that 'It was a time when life, for the class to which the Wyndhams belonged, was easier, better organized, and more brilliant than it had been for a hundred years, or than it has ever been since'. During this time the Wyndham children were growing up, and in themselves they composed a distinguished group. Sargent's picture of the three sisters was more talked about than any picture of the day. It was nicknamed 'the Three Graces' and was reproduced in all the fashionable magazines. In its background the painter introduced an impression of Watts's portrait of Mrs. Wyndham herself, thus suggesting the sustained link which existed between the family at Clouds and the art of one generation after another during the nineteenth century. But it was not only artists who met at Clouds, although perhaps Mrs. Wyndham found her most kindred spirits among them. Painters, writers, actors, and actresses came, and the parties were outstanding in their day, because then, different sets in society were more apart than now. For Clouds was also a centre of the political world. The Wyndhams' elder son George and his sister Mary, afterwards Lady Wemyss, brought all their friends to Clouds. George Wyndham was the Admirable Crichton of his generation. He was a poet and a lover of books, a magnificent horseman and a fearless rider to hounds, and as the great-grandson of Lord Edward Fitzgerald, it seemed to be his vocation to attempt to bring peace to Ireland. The story of his brave attempt and of its tragic failure do not belong to Clouds, but what does belong is the remarkable group of politicians whom George brought to the house. Arthur Balfour was the most famous, but George Curzon, Alfred Littleton, St. John Brodrick, and many more were to be met with at Clouds during Easter week or in the autumn shooting parties. Wilfred Blunt drove his team of Arabs into the park and camped there. Harry Cust wrote verses. Lovely Lady Talbot or Mrs. Harry Legge played on the piano in the great hall. Margot Tennant's wit flashed and sparkled, for Clouds was a favourite meeting place of that famous group of friends dubbed 'The Souls' by their contemporaries. They were the most interesting people of their day, and Madeline enjoyed hearing and sharing in their conversation which was never more brilliant than in her house. Clouds was a great place for after-dinner games —paper games, acting games, guessing games—all played with so much wit and intelligence that they became forms of art. Mrs. Wyndham seldom played herself. She inspired, appreciated, and enjoyed. Her magnetism had drawn around her this gay, sparkling, intellectual life, and while it pulsated about her, she sat at what she called her 'scrattle table', drawing, painting, making designs for embroidery or for her enamels. Her hands were always occupied, but her mind was free, moving among her guests, evoking and kindling. Her paintings and designs were all large in conception, even when the space to be used was restricted, but she hated things to be 'finicky', and she used to criticize the governesses' carefully executed pieces of embroidery because they were too 'tight'.

What made Madeline Wyndham the perfect hostess was that she really possessed a catholic love for the human race. She found a village festivity as enjoyable as a London party, and this was not merely because she was sympathetic enough to throw herself into the spirit of her guests, however humble. A fête at East Knoyle was described in her letters as enthusiastically as the most brilliant society function. When her daughter, Madeline Adeane, was on her honeymoon, she received a graphic account of the Clouds school feast.

'More than two hundred children came, and we had it all very much like last year, only *better* in some ways—more toys and the band was extra, and a *splendid* scramble, a bun and a pear given to each child on arrival. Tea at four-thirty. Races, three-legged, sack, and ordinary races. A bag of sweets and nuts, and a bun on going away. . . . I got a great quantity of toys, reins, trumpets, and musical instruments, flags, balls, hoops, skipping ropes, and all the old ones of last year, so every child had something to play with, three footballs, and two sets of cricket, with stumps, bats, and balls. It looked *too* delicious, and the day kept very fine. *All* the tenants came to see the children, and walked about the green river and garden, and sat in the hall, where Pamela sang to them with gusto. . . . We had a splendid band. . . . The *élite* danced on the Red Pavement and the children in the park.'

Although she was surrounded by so many interesting people, she was never bored by even the most humdrum of country neighbours. Indeed, in her presence nobody *was* hum-drum. She found unexpected gifts in unexpected people. She had brought to her Wiltshire home the talents of her ancestresses, the great French *salonières* of the eighteenth century, and like them she knew how to draw people out and make them at their best, although she never kept the centre of the stage for herself. From the moment when her guests stepped over her threshold to be taken to her heart and to be made free of her circle, they were no more stray individuals, but living members of the world in which she lived and moved.

After his first visit to Clouds, Sir Oliver Lodge wrote a letter to Mrs. Wyndham in the train on his way home:

'My heart is warm and glowing with a sense of kindness and friendship. What a visit! Every minute full of occupation and interest, and delightfully sympathetic conversation. The fabric of your house may be beautiful, but the human fabric is still more beautiful, and the one is a fitting setting for the other. No wonder Mr. Balfour likes to come to you for his Easter, and I had splendid talks with him also . . . To come into your atmosphere is a boon and delight and refreshment, not only for those who belong to you but even to the stranger who feels no longer strange or outside.'

This overflowing love of Madeline Wyndham's reached its climax in her passionate mother love. When she sat down to write to one of her children, there was generally much to tell, of the places she had seen and the people she had been with, for her life was always full with breathless interests and occupations. But what always seemed new and exciting to her, and what streamed most freely from her pen, was her ardent love for the son or the daughter who opened the particular letter she was writing at the moment. All her letters to her family were love-letters. Here are a few lines from one:

'I am just going to bed but must write a line to my own darling child, for it seems very sad that I should leave London the very day that *you* return to it. But such is life, and it does not really matter. We love each other too much for absence to do aught but increase our love. . . . *Oh dear me*, how I wish we could all live together! I don't know *what I shall do* when Guy goes to India. I feel every day the room gets smaller by a window, like the old story, and there is no *getting out of it.*'

In a letter written by George Wyndham to Edward Clifford we can get some impression of how this love was reciprocated by her children. It was written after Mr. Clifford had been to Clouds, and had written his impression of Mrs. Percy Wyndham.

September 1895.

My dear Clifford,

It was good of you to send me the private impression. At first, let me say frankly, I shrank from making any comment; partly because the subject is too dear to me, but mainly because it is, and has ever been at once too large and too inscrutable. It is as if you asked me to comment on an impression of summer or of the west wind. From that sentence you will gauge my difficulty and the reasonable nature of my reluctance. To show what I feel, I should have to write a poem and one of the greatest poems. You would in your turn comment and say, 'In the first place this is a bad poem, and in the second place, I did not want a poem good, bad, or indifferent; but nicely balanced assent and dissent from and to my comparisons and contrasts and conclusions'. Now that is just what I cannot do. The subject is too dear, too large, too intimate, too sacred; you yourself note 'an extraordinary pre-eminence as to desirability' and then hesitate, feeling the difficulty of analysis and setting aside not quite confidently the explanation based on an 'aura'. But that is my explanation. It came to me once in a dream of such vivid intensity (at first excruciating but then happy in a lighthearted and large-hearted sort of way) that I woke bathed in tears and yet smiling and wrote it down. That was years ago, and I have not the description by me. Roughly and briefly it was this. I dreamt that my mother was dying. I held her hand and Sibell was in the room. I felt the horror of her large life-giving life being shut in closer and farther from me, minute by minute, as approaching death paralysed her faculties. I longed till my heart seemed about to break, for any signal of intelligence. But she died and the desolation was intolerable and *she was not there after death.* She had vanished: and, at that instant, I felt her presence more imminent and enveloping than at any moment in my life. She was communicating with me though I heard nothing and saw nothing. Yet through some channel other and larger than those of the sense, all that one does ever hear or see of the beautiful and fresh and high-hearted seemed to be pouring through me like a high wind on a sunlit day, sweeping over the grasses and pouring through the foliage of waving trees. She became an 'aura', a wind sweeping rhythmically over a laughing but lovely landscape where there was no confinement. And as it blew on, herds and troops and cavalcades, first of fair wild animals, deer and the like, then of horsemen, came lilting and galloping in a rhythm of joyous delight, going with the wind. I knew that I was not seeing or hearing. I was being swept through and yet borne on, by a musical fugue of animated pageantry. And I knew that she was not *making* this; but that it was *her*. And I woke, as I said, with my cheek wet with tears but laughing, the words 'What a poet you are!' That was a dream full of fancy, as dreams are. But I could not write now, when very wide awake, without being fanciful.

Certainly she is not 'clever' like Lady Londonderry, my hostess.

Mrs. Percy Wyndham

I think her always very beautiful and sometimes very witty. But humour not wit is her characteristic in the lighter vein. In the sadder vein, she is sympathetic but never pathetic. For she is always generous—I want to say 'generosa' in Latin—magnanimous, always a giver, a fountain of inexhaustible vitality. That, I think, is really the point. Other people by their 'gifts' so called of beauty and cleverness seem to *ask*. It is you have to give. Their beauty and cleverness is exhausting if beautiful; it is not that they are vain, that is, greedy of admiration. There are such. But I am thinking not of them but of her peers, who, though not vain, put a tax on your aesthetic perceptions so that they tire you like a great picture or statue. And again, if clever, they do not seek to demonstrate your ignorance, but they put a tax on your knowledge. I have known really clever women who for purposes of intercourse are a desert that would swallow the Nile to give back not one blade of grass. The point about my mother is that she is always giving just what you want in order to give in your turn. Her gift is not consoling but fructifying. It ignores deficiency and elicits profusion. She is rain to the dry and sunshine to the cheerless for the purpose of producing crops. She has the serenity of climate with the variability of the weather, but of weather that is always opportune. People in her presence feel like trees or birds at their best, singing or flourishing according to their natures with an easy exuberance. This may seem too pleasant and nothing more; as if her influence were not sufficiently elevating. To that I would reply that she never seems to be consciously helping, still less lifting others. That would argue a consciousness of their being down and a confidence of her ability to lift. But there is no arrogance in her and apparently no perception of other people's failings. Yet she helps these, most of all; unconsciously, as a mountain helps those whose horizon is too confined by leading them to lift up their eyes. It is all one to her, whether any has fallen by his own fault or, from no fault of his own, is travelling through one of those sunless gorges of life which we have all at times to traverse. In either case they are unconsciously led to lift up their eyes and after that, to lift up their hearts; so that she is a 'sursum corda'. Sometimes the bravest feel that they are shut in by doors closed fast for ever. Then her presence is an incantation which sings with the voice of the wind 'Lift up your heads, ye everlasting doors, that the King of Glory may enter in'. God to her is, I think, pre-eminently the 'King of Glory', and she has a peculiar gift for making this world glorious to all who meet her in it.

I warned you that I should have to be fanciful if I wrote at all.

Yours ever,

GEORGE WYNDHAM.

One more 'character sketch' from another letter written by a guest at Clouds, in the year 1905:

'It was a delightful visit, and made me feel afresh that the extraordinary pre-eminence of M.W. as to desirability as a companion is not a mistake. She is endowed—I have always imagined it—with that gift that secures to everyone in her company the gift of unaccustomed happiness. Everyone basks in her presence, and is at more than his, or her, best. They leave her with enthusiastic admiration, and exalted in their own opinion of themselves. I cannot altogether account for it, nor, I am sure, could she. One great point is that all effort is banished in her presence. We forget to *try* to make ourselves pleasant or useful. We are at our best, and somehow get a chance to shine. Every single person feels this, old or young, clever or stupid, bad or good. In her presence there is a tendency not to think of ourselves, but to be engrossed with something to be done, and to come away enriched.

This absence of effort is a great and unique point in her atmosphere. She has an exceptionally generous nature. Her largesse is unrestrained, and surpasses the imagination of the most clamative person. If there is a scent that is like her, it is the sweet briar—a delicious, homely fragrance. She is not (as some people have suggested) at all like a magnolia. It is much too luxurious, and overwhelming, and wealthy for her. She is never overwhelming. Her taste is perfect as to poetry, flowers, decoration, pictures, houses, garden. She is distinctly humble, and never realizes or thinks of her virtues. She is an admiring mother, and an appreciative friend. I imagine that her servants rise up and call her blessed. The light of her penetrates in all directions. She has become increasingly religious as years have passed on. Her religious views are very sane.

Mrs. Percy Wyndham

Her kindness subordinates even her humour, so that an unkind word, even if it be witty, gives her little pleasure. How many people we talked of during that visit! All her children, of course, and many friends. . . . We painted half the time, and walked, or read, or listened. As one would expect, she ages beautifully, as flowers do. She moves a little more slowly than formerly, her radiance is softer, with more of Heaven about it. She is, I think about sixty-eight. The house is generous, and full of beautiful things. All the Watts portraits framed, many flowers (Curtis) and birds (Japanese); fine Morris pictures, beautiful Burne-Jones drawings. Many of us have just a touch of priggishness. She never had, not for one moment, not once in her life. She is more kind than philanthropic, more good than virtuous, more delightful than brilliant. Her disapproval is unwilling, but it is never dissembled, for to dissemble it would neutralize its opposites. Her friendships are a great deal to her. The scheme of her character is planned on such large lines that, if anything, she has been bored by being too much admired.'

Nothing is oftener said nowadays than that this war will be the end of the great English country houses of the past. The thought evokes different reactions in different minds; but there can be little doubt, if those houses do disappear, there will disappear with them much of the culture of the past five centuries. Merely as buildings, they are the incarnation of the artistic genius of one generation after another throughout the great age of English architecture. If they perish, there will perish with them the hope of maintaining an English tradition in the buildings of the future. A new style in any art must be aware of what has gone before even if it only shows its awareness by rejecting the old clichés. This awareness proves its right to be in any way civilized or educated art. The great houses of England stand throughout the length and breadth of the land as outward and visible signs of the art and culture of the past. And architecture is the one form of visual art with which the country people can have personal acquaintance.

More than this. All over Europe the great houses have been the centres from which the civilization we know spread slowly over the lands which had once been united under the Roman Empire. It was nurtured in the country houses of the aristocracy. The ladies of the Italian Renaissance gathered round them the artists and poets of their day. *The Courtier* of Castiglione describes the court of Elizabeth Gonzaga, Duchess of Urbino, and from that we know what other courts were like. The poetic constellation of the Pleiades sparkled round the Queen of Navarre. In this country, we hear in Queen Elizabeth's day of 'the College' which Mary Sidney assembled at Wilton and from which there issued the *Arcadia* written by her famous brother, Sir Philip Sidney. The little German courts of the eighteenth century were the soil from which grew the musical genius of Bach and Mozart and the poetry of Goethe. At the same time, the Whig aristocracy of England was not only building the great English country houses, but was nurturing within them the public spirit of country gentlemen who sustained in this country the tradition that politics was a noble career for the cultured and patriotic patrician.

This tradition lived on at Clouds when Mr. and Mrs. Percy Wyndham gathered round themselves the best minds of their day in politics, literature, and the arts. And now, the estate of Clouds has become a Garden City for the intelligentsia.

'All gone. Alas! Alas!'